Know Thyself

by

Richard Lynch

NITY BOOKS • LEE'S SUMMIT, MO.

Know Thyself

was first published in 1935.

This is the tenth printing.

U NITY IS A link in the great educational movement inaugurated by Jesus Christ; our objective is to discern the truth in Christianity and prove it. The truth that we teach is not new, neither do we claim special revelations or discovery of new religious principles. Our purpose is to help and teach mankind to use and prove the eternal Truth taught by the Master.—*Charles Fillmore, founder of Unity*

CONTENTS

IN APPRECIATION

I should like to take advantage of this opportunity, for surely no better occasion will be afforded me, to say a word of appreciation.

At this moment, I am glancing backward to the time when I first met Charles and Myrtle Fillmore, founders of Unity School. That introduction was a momentous occasion for me, as it definitely changed the entire course of my life. Eagerly was I in quest of Truth, and grateful was I to find so pure a source of spiritual and scientific interpretation as these great and good teachers. To them and to their vast work do I ever pour out my deepest appreciation.

RICHARD LYNCH

NEW YORK

Knowledge of Truth

THERE IS AN ESTABLISHED FOUNDATION on which every premise and every problem must be based. It is the fixed reality that is uncompromising, unyielding, and unchangeable. It is the thing that is, the only thing we can know, the criterion by which every act and feeling and condition is measured. We speak of it glibly as Truth, but when we are asked to define it we find ourselves sympathizing with the bewilderment of Pilate when he asked his immortal question "What is truth?"

We shall never understand the meaning of Truth until we come to know what God is, because it is the vision we perceive through soul insight. It is the ultimate, illimitable, infinite power pervading all existence. It is the hidden harmony of life; the single thread of meaning that runs through and connects all things; the unchangeable principle that controls the universe.

"To this end am I come into the world, that I should bear witness unto the truth." Such was the declaration of the greatest prisoner who ever stood at the bar of what men call justice. No drama has ever reached such stirring heights as this tragic episode in the life of the Galilean. No trial scene ever ended in such a climactic finale as the question that proclaimed the indecision of an unwilling and unconvinced judge. "What is truth?" Thus was brought to a close the judicial examination of Jesus.

Pilate was responsible to Rome for the enforcement
of law and order. Outside the courtroom the mob
clamored loudly for a death sentence on the prisoner.
The people were fast becoming unmanageable and
were threatening violence. Before him stood the
man in whom Pilate could "find no fault," the man
who claimed to bear witness to Truth at the very
time when He was being accused of perverting it.
Very likely this Roman politician had encountered
other such paradoxical situations. He can scarcely
be blamed for his agitated query "What is truth?"

It would seem that everybody knows what Truth
is, yet Pilate's troubled question has echoed and re-
echoed down the centuries and is still perplexing
those who, like the Roman governor, are not of the
Truth. Religion claims to know the answer. Philosophy would solve the problem. Science works
untiringly over its interpretation. The explanations
often clash. We surmise and believe many errors,
but Truth remains always the same. Man changes,
Truth does not. It stands as firm and as immutable
as God. It demonstrates itself and is its own de-
fense. As man realizes and accepts it he learns to
understand all the qualities and attributes of God
as changeless and eternal, "the same yesterday and
today, *yea* and for ever."

"Things that are equal to the same thing are
equal to each other" is an axiom we all have learned.
Having all the attributes of God, Truth is equal to
God, or the same as God. Both are ultimate, infinite, and illimitable. As such man does not know

them very intimately, yet there is something within him that is ever urging him onward to a solution that will satisfy his longing for attainment. And this urge is never really satisfied with anything less than absolute Truth.

Life is continually getting out of adjustment. Men are continually puzzling themselves over the question "What is the reality of this condition or problem?" Material states are always changing, just as beliefs and opinions vary. But Principle remains. There is always the law of Truth to which we may conform. It is the reality or the idea of the thing itself. Seeing it corrects material misconceptions and "trues up" race beliefs.

The laws of mathematics are founded on principles that few of us would care to dispute or contest. They constitute the bases of physics and chemistry and astronomy; of music and architecture and art. In business they are absolutely essential. The man who digs a well or builds a wall must use a plummet to make both "true." The merchant who sells goods must back them up as genuine, or lose his reputation for reliability. Truth is the cornerstone of trade upon which the relations of buyer and seller must be founded. A man's word is expected to be "as good as his bond." The law demands truth of witnesses in court trials; they are sworn to "tell the truth, the whole truth, and nothing but the truth." On this principle only can justice be upheld between man and man. Twice two is four is a mathematical truth. Perfectly working mechanical devices and correctly surveyed lands are engineering truths. A bridge must be constructed truly. Purity in material is the guarantee of the builder's integrity. The very foundation stone of nature is Truth, and no enduring success can be achieved without it.

We expect truthfulness in our friends, and it is a distressing discovery to find our trust betrayed. It is hard to forgive even those little deviations from veracity known as "white lies," which are often used to protect us from anxiety. It troubles us to find a child telling an untruth, and we study to correct what is back of it. A malicious lie is cruel, dangerous, and deadly, and may result in frightful catastrophe. Untold harm has been done to the world through intellectual dishonesty. In speaking of a man who has been highly praised for his knowledge, an American humorist remarked, "Yes, he knows a great many things, but most of them aren't true."

"Be sure you are right, then go ahead," we have been taught. But how are we to know what is right? Everywhere we hear controversies on the subject. Wars are fought with each side claiming the championship of God because its cause is right. Political parties promise their constituents the only "right" kind of legislation. Each religious denomination claims the one and only right road to salvation. Scientists struggle over relative and absolute laws. In all these groups and individuals there seems to exist such a positive assurance of right, even when they have not made Truth the basis of their assertions. Nothing is right if it cannot stand the test of Truth. Truth is always right, and Truth is unchangeable. It cannot be altered to fit the opinions or beliefs or desires of men.

In a metaphysical sense, Truth is often difficult to understand, since it deals with much that is speculative. Yet there are things that are transcendental. In Christianity we speak of the teachings of Jesus as spiritual Truth. Even though we may be unable to demonstrate them, we instinctively recognize in them the perfect accuracy of the one Mind in which we may trace the relationship both of ideas to one another and of ideas to the mind. When religion becomes established on Truth; when it is accounted for, classified, and demonstrated as such, there will be no more friction regarding creeds and dogmas. Absolute Truth will be firmly fixed in the consciousness of man.

The ultimate aim of each individual is to gain a consciousness of Truth. In this knowledge man finds himself and the particular work he is intended to do. Each man brings a gift into the world, a donation to its progress. Each is restless and unsatisfied until he has delivered his contribution. He becomes free from the ignorance that binds and hampers him only in proportion to his knowledge of Truth. False thinking makes his way hard, but Truth is always liberating. It relieves man of his responsibility by establishing God as the one Mind. Man thinks in terms of the Mind in which he has his being. His only responsibility is to know Truth. If he thinks according to spiritual principles he is thinking the way God thinks, and he may cast all his responsibilities upon Divine Mind. He shall know the Truth and the Truth shall set him free.

In trying to work out a mathematical problem without a knowledge of what rules to apply, our result is almost bound to be incorrect. We must not only believe in the law, we must know it. We have to know Truth in its spiritual dominion before it can set us free from error. Our various opinions about it cannot affect its calm imperturbability. Truth is, just as God is. It always was, it is now, and it always will be. It is the alpha and omega, the beginning and the end. Our acceptance or rejection of it neither influences nor changes it. We are the ones who are affected. In its name many persecutions and atrocities have been perpetrated. Men have believed or disbelieved strange things about it. It remains firm and secure in its perfection and in its ability to meet every demand made upon it.

A mathematical rule is a measure of Truth by which each problem is worked out. We get a right or wrong answer as we know and apply the specific principle to its corresponding proposition. A spiritual law is also a measure of Truth for the solution of problems. Success or failure in life depends on knowledge and use of principle. Ignorance of law does not excuse the lawbreaker. Perversion of Truth works out according to law. Human weakness and failure do not influence it. Two and two does not make five, even though many tears may be shed over the fact.

Truth cannot be bent to fit human emotions and desires. They must conform to it. What men have believed and written and preached about God has not changed Him in the least. None of these things has altered the absolute Truth, which both stabilizes the universe and relates it to God. The Supreme Being has been many different things to many different minds. As we read our Scriptures we see how human opinions of Him have changed. Old Testament accounts make Him out as angry, jealous, vindictive, fickle, and prejudiced by turns. Jesus changed this entire meaning by naming Him love. We are fast learning today to regard Him as omnipotent Principle, or absolute Truth.

Old ideas persist, however, and men still bow down before Him in fear and humility. They still implore Him to give them their desires, to change His attitude toward them, and to reconcile them to the sorrows and losses they feel He has thrust upon them as punishments. They want God to walk with them; they do not want to walk with Him. They would be "sons of this world," yet they seek to divert Truth into channels of materiality by trying to cajole God into setting aside universal law.

The human idea of prayer is hard to change. The idea of humble petitioning clings to it. But effective prayer means harmony with undeviating, established Truth through our thinking about man and the universe as God holds them in His consciousness. The Truth of His creation—its spiritual reality—is perfection. Discord and imperfection

cannot exist in His realm. They should not exist in
man's consciousness, because in reality man has always been the divine son of God, a perfect expression of the Father. Outside of Truth there can
be no real existence, but material beliefs will obscure man's perception until he is able to look beyond them and understand the futility of human
opinions.

The declaration of every divine son should be
"I came into the world to bear witness unto Truth."
The purpose of each individual should be triumph
of Principle. In the conscious realization of Principle all sin and disease would be healed; they are
but distorted shadows resulting from incorrect vision.
As such, they would cease to be if the blazing calcium
light of Truth were focused on them. Knowledge
of Truth restores man to the harmony of Divine
Mind and the consequent adjustment of all his affairs.

Earth is a limited state of immature thought.
Insight into Truth is a consciousness of perfection,
which is heaven. Man may live on the earth, yet not
be of it. To the extent that he perceives Truth he
dwells in heaven. His consciousness is changed at
the very moment of this perception. Whatever the
error may be, it is corrected and bodied forth as
healing or adjustment. As long as a misconception
remains, its corresponding inharmony will persist.

Failure to see and interpret Truth results in false-
hood and misrepresentation. In itself, wrong is
simply lack of Truth, a negative condition. It can

easily be changed from an appearance of disaster into a miraculous proof of the orderly, systematic intelligence that is behind universal Truth. But until man does comprehend the principle he can neither interpret nor represent it. He must know it before he can work out its results in his life.

The knowledge that man is a spiritual being and that creation was first a spiritual concept sets us free from all human error and finite sense of limitation. In the beginning, when God saw His divine plan of creation, He pronounced it very good. In reality, which is the consciousness of the Creator, it has never been otherwise; it never can be anything less than perfect. When man can rise above material delusions and sense beliefs and behold the Truth, he will see, as God sees, that all is "very good." But as long as he believes in the reality of matter he will remain bound with the shackles of the race.

"Ye shall know the truth, and the truth shall make you free." How the Jews of that age resented this statement of Jesus! How they objected to any idea of bondage! How men still resent anything that interferes with their personal liberty or freedom of individual expression! And how little they yet understand what the Master meant by either "truth" or freedom!

Truth is the divine emancipator, however humble it may be. It has changed man's belief in many errors. It has given him the freedom of land and sea and air. It will accomplish vastly more than this when he demonstrates its emancipation of spirit.

each small overcoming

Perfection is the final goal toward which creation is advancing. Each man's perception of Truth in himself speeds up the momentum of the process as a whole. Each man's discovery necessitates the elimination of accumulated false opinions and beliefs which he has been harboring as realities. As he yields himself to the guidance of the Spirit of truth, it will lead him into all Truth. To the extent that he allows it, Spirit sets him free from illusions of sense and their hampering effects.

We look to Jesus as the great teacher of Truth. His words were Truth. He received them from the source of all Truth. We follow His teaching because we recognize its genuine ring as surely as we know the ring of pure metal. A man who stands upon the rock of Truth cannot be broken. Jesus' Truth will prevail long after His words are forgotten. Through the simple words of Jesus a great light shone, a light that has illumined the world for many centuries. This was an eternal light because it was kindled with the divine spark of Truth. This radiance illumines our daily life so that we see a truer way of doing our work, better opportunities for advancement, finer inspiration for development.

meditation

Many problems confront us today. Let us begin right now to let this light shine on them. It will dissolve them as misty shadows are scattered in the sun's radiance. Let us know that Truth is always the unchangeable criterion by which our lives must be measured and tried.

First Principle

YEAR BY YEAR MAN is coming closer to the
secret of the universe. Day by day he is learning more about the great principle, the intelligent power that holds cosmos back from chaos.
Without the inspiration of the great principle of
law and order there would be no universe. It is
upheld in a way we do not yet fully understand, by
something we can neither see nor define. We only
know that it exists, and that its principle is inviolate.
It is a spirit of orderly purpose moving everywhere,
in the least as well as in the greatest of its creations.
It is in man as well as in what we call nature. This
incomprehensible, yet ever-present ruling intelligence
is God.

To every person who thinks deeply there comes
a time when he is brought face to face with the question "What is God? and what does He mean to me?"
That He must mean something is inevitable. We
can find no comfort in seeking to dismiss the subject altogether, nor can we be happy so long as we
are torn by doubt and uncertainty. What we think
about God, whether consciously or subconsciously,
influences everything that we think about ourselves
and one another, about living and learning and loving. He is the great meaning of the universe and of
our individual existence.

Probably the designation of God as Father is
largely responsible for the personal God of the child

17

mind. This mind has clothed Him with parent attributes on a large scale and has thus kept Him anthropomorphic. How many Gods have come down to us as legacies of the past! How many ideas of Him, colored by the minds in which they took form and shape! A just God, whose dominant principle was an eye for an eye, and who meted out punishment accordingly. A loving God, too kind to be altogether just! A changeable God, now giving, now withholding. An angry God, destroying and laying waste. A jealous God, demanding sacrifice and service. A God to be feared and obeyed, loved, flattered and praised, implored, and cajoled.

The wisest thing we can do is to abolish, once and forever, all these man-made conceptions of deity, and to give some attention to a creation of our own; to ask ourselves, "What does God mean to me?" When I turn the brilliant calcium of Truth on these products of other men's imagination, what do I find that appeals to me? My idea of God may not be yours, nor yours mine. No one has a right to impose his interpretation upon another in the form of belief or creed or dogma. Even God does not force Himself upon us; that part of Him which was placed within man "in the beginning" has its power of choice, which is an attribute of God.

One of the most imaginative dramatic presentations the stage has ever given us is Sutton Vane's play, performed several years ago, dealing with the subject of life after death. In this play, "Outward Bound," a sorely troubled soul cries out for advice in making his decision, but he is told that no one can help him; the choice must be his own. After he has chosen, however, all the assistance he has been imploring instantly comes to him. We find life startlingly like that. As long as we grope vaguely about, seeking the ideas and opinions of others, we are lost in a maze of indecision. But once we have decided and taken our stand, immediately there comes flooding in upon us a perfect deluge of all that we have been so earnestly desiring.

decision

The attempt to reduce God to modern terms sometimes proves to be the first step toward eliminating Him altogether; and yet it is my belief that no person can really do that. Men may be uneasy at the mention of His name. They may even call themselves agnostics and atheists, but it is usually because they have been unable to banish from their minds one or more of the old, outworn conceptions that theology has bequeathed to us. To say that we do not believe anything that we experience today is to acknowledge a certain amount of ignorance regarding it.

No one would think of denying the existence of electricity because we have never seen it and can give no intelligent definition of it. We know that it is, although we are unable to tell what it is. Even the most skeptical must admit that there is a spirit in man; but can he define it? It is as vague as the breath of the wind, yet we know that without it the body is dead.

That God is spirit was the teaching of Jesus; and

God must be spiritually discerned. We cannot measure Him by our human limitations. How is it that
we really know one another? Not by form or feature
or coloring: these are subject to change. It is only
as we perceive in another the spirit that responds to
our own—the inner "something" that is attuned to
our own individual keynote—that we appreciate its
true reality.

"To whom then will ye liken God? or what likeness will ye compare unto him?" Men are thus
continuing to voice the cry of the prophet Isaiah
in their attempts to solve the Infinite. So many
images of Him! Yet they can all be resolved into
one simple truth. Back of all theological doctrine,
back of primitive fear, back of devotion and sacrifice and supplication lies the basic idea of a power
greater than man's, a "something" on which he re-
lies and calls when his puny human efforts fail. It
is a truth that is real, a principle that is dependable,
a love that is immutable, a good that is immeasur-
able, a life that is eternal. This new vision of God
sometimes brings the desolate feeling that He has
been taken away from us altogether, yet we know
that, in reality, it has brought Him very close and
made Him infinitely greater than any old conception
that we may have had regarding Him as a personality.

It is of no great importance that we should call
this power God. The fact that we feel dependent
on it proves our belief in it. Many a man has taken
his first step toward this belief over the shattered
images of other men's Gods. Many a blind be-

lief, stumbled on in an hour of dire need, has developed through experience into understanding faith; faith in a spirit of good from which man's being has been derived and on which he may eternally rely. We establish an inner contact with this power as we give our attention to it. Because all do not make the same contacts, men have dared to judge and punish and kill one another in the name of their conceptions of God, which each has arrogantly assumed to be the only correct one.

Voltaire, whose name is associated with all manner of infidelities, yet pronounced the aphorism that it would be necessary to invent God if He did not exist. Not many years ago the name of Robert Ingersoll was seriously interdicted—in fact, it was considered sacrilegious even to mention him. Yet today we know that he had contact with God through an appreciation of the beauty of the divine qualities in humanity. Shortly before the passing of Luther Burbank, a great discussion arose concerning his religious beliefs. "Isn't it strange," people said, "that Burbank doesn't believe in God!" And the religious beliefs of Thomas A. Edison, often a subject of controversy during his lifetime, still remain indefinite and mysterious to those who place limitations of theological doctrine upon their interpretation of God. Both Burbank and Edison touched God very closely; the one through nature, the other through science. Both continually insisted that of themselves they could do nothing; that they were channels through which intelligence passed. An-

other great man, perhaps the greatest intellectual
of our day, although accused of agnosticism, has expressed his belief in an evolving God. "God in the
act of making Himself constitutes the universe" is
George Bernard Shaw's way of putting it.

God includes all of these conceptions, and what
I think or what you think or what Shaw thinks does
not change the nature of God in the least. But what
each of us thinks changes the nature of our own
existence. God includes all. One kind of contact
with Him does not exclude others. He is—wher-
ever humanity has found Him—in the harmony and
order of growth, in the power and energy of vibration, in the activity and purpose of life, in the joy
and love of Spirit. He is just as little or as much
as we choose to experience in Him. His totality is
as hard for the human mind to comprehend as the
vastness of interstellar space or the infinitesimal
smallness of the atom. Yet there is a spiritual quality within the mind of man that is receptive to divine
understanding and that, when cultivated, intuitively
knows.

God can never be defined in material terms, any
more than we can so define what intelligence is or
what love is or what life is. We know that they
exist and we see evidences of their activities. That
they do exist is proof positive that they must have
a source. We think of that final source as God.
Whatever flows from the fountainhead must par-
take of its qualities. If we think of a man as a channel continually being supplied from the infinite

source, we must understand him to be a partaker of the nature of that source. The channel was an open one in the beginning, but man has blocked it with all sorts of material things. Man himself must remove the barriers before the divine inflow can be resumed. The degree of its ebbing or flowing depends on how thoroughly he has cleared the channel and opened himself to the influx of Spirit.

If man would experience God as his health and life, he must remove the debris of the disease and death thoughts of the race. If he would have Truth, love, and intelligence, he must dredge out lies, hatred, and ignorance. He may, if he so desires, live and move and have his being in God, or he may try to do without Him. He may saturate himself with God, knowing that God is "over all, and through all, and in all," or he may think that he can exclude Him altogether.

Sooner or later, at some moment in his life, every person feels an inadequacy to meet it independently. He cannot escape this, as it is the very nature of man to seek his source of being. Those who have not learned how to do this are the failures and the suicides of the world. Their sense of separation has rendered them hopeless. They have broken the wires that connected them with the power of the universe.

The word "hell" means to separate, to shut off, while "heaven" and "harmony" are synonymous. Hell, then, is a withdrawal from harmonious conditions, a separation from the infinite Principle of or-

derly harmony, a rebellion against universal law
and order. It is the result of seeing through a glass
of sense consciousness a darkly blurred vision of
reality. Seen through this defective medium the
world appears distorted into various ugly shapes that
we call "evil." In itself, evil is nothingness, a result of incorrect seeing, and sin is the consequence
of this abnormal vision—a failure to measure up to
the inherent divinity. "The way of the transgressor
is hard," because he is trying to fly against a head
wind. Everything in the world is co-operating with
the man who has chosen to work with the great
principle of good, but difficulties and obstacles thrust
themselves in the path of sin. Failure to harmonize
with divine Principle brings disturbance into the life
of the individual; for sin and its consequences are
inseparable.

Knowledge and application of Truth, spiritually
discerned, destroy effects by removing their causes.
In working out an idea of wholeness, we experience
God as health; in educating inherent intelligence,
ignorance is banished; in cultivating divine love, we
drive out hate and its long train of attendants known
as jealousy, criticism, condemnation, intolerance, and
gossip; as we gain faith we lose fear; joy counter-
acts sorrow; a conviction of substance abolishes lack
and poverty; confident faith in life—real, abun-
dant, eternal life—overcomes death.

The great central fact on which all these ideas
depend is that there exists a Principle, which is orderly and reliable, which creates and works and rules

for our good as we lay hold of it and harmonize ourselves with it. It is all-powerful and everywhere present, ready to be chosen and employed by us anywhere, at any time, in any degree. Spirit, including as it does, all love, all joy, all faith, all substance, all life, is God.

Each of us is an individual expression of God. We find Him as we become conscious of our at-onement with Him. To the degree that we realize this, we make it possible for Him to express Himself through us. Conscious unity with the Father brings us into a realization of our spiritual inheritance. We have His mind, His life, and His power as we maintain contact with them in Him. When we have thus found and experienced Him we shall know Him as our unfailing resource. We shall never be alone, for His love constantly infolds us.

We may receive from Him continuous draughts of power, manifesting more and more of good in our daily life. We may find Him everywhere, in everything, at any time; in the magnificent coloring of the sunset or in the starry firmament; in a tiny flower or a giant redwood; in the majesty of the hills or the dashing ocean waves; in the comradeship of friends or the quietness of solitude. The heavens declare His glory and the firmament shows His handiwork. Day unto day utters speech of Him, and night unto night shows knowledge of Him. There is no speech nor language where He is not heard.

God may mean just as much to you as you desire.

As you think of Him you experience Him. He may
be your Father, upon whom you rely for all things.
You may find Him as love, joy, or Truth; as life,
mind or Principle; as intelligence, energy, or power;
as one or as all of these things. He is all-inclusive,
and He may mean to you whatever you choose to experience in Him.

Know Thyself

ALL THROUGH the history of philosophy there has persisted an earnest attempt to solve the mystery of man. The oldest of these was the Vedanta of India, which said that nothing is greater than the attainment of a knowledge of the self. The highest wisdom of the ancient Greeks was expressed in but two words, "Know thyself." This precept was inscribed high above the temple doors. The Bible story of man is a record of his spiritual advancement, related in the form of myth and allegory. There is Job pondering his mystic purpose; David typifying his supremacy; Jeremiah denouncing his frailty; Isaiah prophesying his perfection; Jesus embodying His Christ inherency; Paul eulogizing his divinity; and John visioning his glorification. The story of Christianity is an account of man's gradual upward trend; broken at many points, it is true, often seeming to halt or even to slide backward; hampered by creed and dogma, by prejudice and arrogance, by skepticism and criticism. And yet, in the face of all this, man has moved ever upward and onward. In the story of evolution he stands at present at the culmination and holds its trusteeship in his hands. According to the Bible narrative, he was made in the image and likeness of God and given dominion over all things. Thus the same objective is reached. Science and religion are agreed on at least one indisputable fact: man's high estate

27

in the universal plan.

If the fabled gentleman from Mars were to drop in on us today, he might possibly get the impression from our newspapers, our literature, and our films that men are all gangsters and racketeers, thieves and murderers, and that dishonesty and crime, injustice, unemployment, and poverty run riot. But if he were to stay awhile and read beyond the "front page," he would find that the ugly hydra that is just now thrusting its many heads of crime between man and his advancement, is really only a fresh challenge and an opportunity to achieve another rung in the ladder of evolution that humanity is so steadily ascending.

The voice of science speaks clearly and convincingly through Pupin and Millikan, Lodge and Jeans, Eddington and Einstein, and a score of others, declaring that the glory of God is still advancing. And Julian Huxley, from a biological standpoint, sees this glory embodied in man, who although but a mere youth of one hundred thousand years, is always marching on. If by means of his endowment of conscious reason, he will use his increased knowledge in the service of the universal, what goal may he not reach in another hundred thousand years!

What is this man that "doth bestride the narrow world, like a Colossus," and whose spirit reaches toward the stars as surely as the sparks fly upward? Is he, though the product of mutation, any the less the image and likeness of God than the mythical clay figure formed of the dust of the earth and inspired by the almighty breath? There is something in every individual that tells him—or would tell him, if he did but listen—that his life is a derived one, drawn from and sustained by a source greater than just physical matter.

> "The soul that rises with us, our life's star,
>   Hath had elsewhere its setting,
>   And cometh from afar.
>   Not in entire forgetfulness,
>   And not in utter nakedness,
>   But trailing clouds of glory, do we come
>   From God, who is our home."

It is hardly necessary to credit Wordsworth with these lines. The quotation is too well known and loved to need classifying. He has been called the poet of nature, and through nature he has discerned that man is the son or expression of divine Principle; a manifestation of Being; the embodiment of a perfect ideal held always in the thought of God. "All things whatsoever the Father hath" have been entrusted to His keeping. He is a steward of Divine Mind, a channel through which God power flows into manifestation. He has been given dominion over all things, including himself, in that he is free to choose his own destiny. His strength lies in his perception of his dependence on the universal, and his necessity of co-operating with it. He is the custodian of evolution, with the privilege of speeding up its progress toward a realization of the divine ideal.

the truth of our Being [handwritten marginal note]

The spirit of man is ever yearning to express the divine image that was stamped upon his soul "in the beginning." If he will but co-operate with this urge he may accomplish wondrous things. Those who close their consciousness to it are unable to understand its meaning. Words cannot describe the divine impulse. To be realized it must be experienced. The man who recognizes it as the voice of the Creator within himself, and who combines its ideas with those of his individual mind, makes of himself a new and particular creation, and may truly claim his relationship with divine Principle. The continuous, insistent impetus he feels is the God-Mind thinking through its image and likeness and seeking to express itself in distinctive embodiment. It functioned perfectly through Jesus and expressed the Christ or immaculate sonship.

It is a far cry from the old teaching that regarded man as a poor worm of the dust, born in sin and iniquity, to trouble and resignation, to the realization of him as a necessary factor in the expression of God. Yet every human being is eligible to divine sonship. As his intelligence increases, man is bound to leave behind him antiquated ideas that were once established convictions. A person who today believed that the earth is flat or that electricity is a product of witchcraft would be subjected to jeering ridicule. But many children are still taught that God is a great, invisible person to be feared and worshiped; to be conciliated with praise and cajoled into forgiving our natural inheritance of sin; and who is to admit us finally into the fabled city of the blessed. And men continue to repeat the prayer of supplication for deliverance from divine wrath and vengeance.

The teaching of Jesus has been bent and compressed and constricted to fit into an antiquated outline of ignorance. But this new era is gradually coming to realize that the Nazarene was born many years in advance of His time. The great central truth of His message was the incarnation of the Christ consciousness in man: God, the Father or intrinsic principle of man, and man, the son or expression of God.

One of the oldest doctrines of philosophy analyzed the nature of man into three distinct functions of being: spirit, soul, and body. The body is the sum total of what man has believed about it. It is thought personified, consciousness objectified. The natural or physical body is that which the sense man has perceived; it is an inheritance of the race consciousness. It is born, lives, and dies after the manner of its heritage of material belief. This has branded it as mortal and destructible. It is never the true body imaged by eternal Principle. Physical science is beginning to teach that there is no real reason for the deterioration of the body. Scientists declare that it has recuperative powers and rejuvenating elements which make it capable of indefinite renewal. They are continually seeking the secret that shall lead to triumph over the dread enemy, death.

We speak of the "likeness" that is imaged by immutable Principle as the spiritual body of man and

the fulfillment of the divine ideal. This is the true
body, ethereal and indestructible. It is the reality
that each man's inner being tells him that he should
manifest and thus trample death under his feet. It
is the discovery the scientist works tirelessly to reveal. His efforts are futile because he employs only
physical energies in its solution, while the real or
deathless man is a spiritual conception. In this connection we realize more than ever that Jesus lived
far in advance of His time. He was the great exemplification of the spiritual or Lord's body. He taught
that this body could also be achieved by others, but
His teaching was too radical for that age. Failing
to comprehend its real significance, men perverted it
to mean a resurrection of the soul. Death had so obsessed the race consciousness that even those who
had been eye witnesses of Jesus' victory over it, gradually lost their conviction of a resurrection of the
body. But we are living in an era of change, and
though death still obsesses the race mind, the miraculous does not seem so impossible as it once did.
Evolution is approaching ever nearer to its goal,
which the intuition of man tells him must be the
redemption of the body. He is even now proving
thought energy to be the fountain of youth, health,
and substance. He must clear his human mind of
all barriers of racial inheritance; he must cast out of
it that natural body which has so hampered his advancement with its convictions of pain, disease, and
death. The Lord's body is a finished product. It has
always been what it will finally become. The divine

son of God must one day see it "face to face."

The modern metaphysician interprets spirit, soul, and body as mind, idea, and expression. To Jesus it was the way, the Truth, and the life; and Paul, in one of his brilliant letters to the Thessalonians, stated it thus: "The God of peace himself sanctify you wholly; and may your spirit and soul and body be preserved entire." This whole man, the real or inmost self of him—the *atman* of the Vedanta, the I AM of Scripture, the *Christ* of Jesus is the "son" or "perfect-man" idea of God. In reality he is but one and he exists eternally in the mind of the Father. Each individual is originally an expression of this ideal, and in his true state he should function equally well on all planes of being, the spiritual, the mental, and the physical.

While of himself man can accomplish nothing, as he is but a channel through which omnipotent Principle flows, he has been given the individual power of choice, and may elect to function on one or all of his planes of consciousness, as he sees fit. The majority choose a great deal of the physical and just enough of the mental to "get by" with, neglecting the spiritual altogether. Others accentuate either the mental or the spiritual at the expense of the other two. It is fatal to become fanatical on the subject of overdeveloping any one of the three, with a consequent disregard of those which complete the trinity. The perfect, harmonious relationship among the three, which exists in Divine Mind, is what man should work to attain. When he recognizes this

fact and makes it a part of his conscious being, he
has found the secret of his divine lineage. His work
is to reveal through his sonship the attributes of his
Father. Otherwise his life is meaningless. His failure to express his Father's perfection is no proof that
it does not exist. It merely indicates his own inability to carry out the expression.

In the mind of God there is held eternally the
perfect triune model of man, immortal and unchangeable, spirit, soul, and body. Every individual
has inherited, potentially, the mind of his Creator.
But like the prodigal son in the parable, he is not
compelled to remain in his Father's house. He may
take his inheritance and go into a far country. He
may squander his riches for material things and feed
on the empty husks of the consequent effects. Or he
may work with and for his Father and be ever with
Him, sharing all that He has. But he must not resent the return of the repentant brother, for the
Father's welcome always awaits him who "was dead
[to Principle], and is alive [to it] *again; and was*
lost, and is found."

> "Man's inhumanity to man
>   Makes countless thousands mourn,"

wrote Scotland's poet. Those countless thousands
are rapidly diminishing as civilization and culture
are taking the place of barbarism and self-interest.
The Golden Rule is proving its practicality in all
situations and under all conditions of living. Hu-

man relationships are fast being readjusted and established on a principle of brotherhood, as men come to realize the futility of disagreement and hatred. If a man cannot love his brother whom he has seen, how then shall he love God whom he has not seen? And certainly no man can recognize his own divine sonship while denying it to his fellow man. Jesus made it very clear that every individual is responsible for the adjustment not only of his grievance against his brother, but of his brother's grievance against him. It is only as we perceive the divine image in another that we establish it in ourselves. We must recognize its potentiality even though it may seem utterly lost in indifference or selfishness or vice or crime. It requires the persistence of divine love to uncover the spiritual reality that exists somewhere in every son of the Father; but no man can be worthy of his royal inheritance until he sees humanity as it eternally exists in the mind of God, glorified by virtue of its divine sonship.

The great, orderly principle that upholds and sustains the universe, that directs and controls the natural world, is ever at man's command, ready to help him work out the mystery of his being. His point of contact is mind. When he thinks according to principle he touches the God ideal of man, and sees his own real self as the perfect son of a perfect Father. He thus follows out the edict of the Master "Ye therefore shall be perfect, as your heavenly Father is perfect." As man establishes this fact in his consciousness, it must, according to immutable

law, be expressed in his body and affairs; for behind
it lies the inexhaustible force of Omnipotence.

Jesus taught that man must be born again before
his divine inheritance can be made manifest. One
of the scholars of Jesus' day voiced the question of
the ages, "How can these things be?" The problem
has had various answers and misinterpretations.
Rightly understood it is clearly evident that Jesus
spoke of the awakening, in the soul, of the Christ
consciousness, of the conviction of the immaculate
conception of the real or ideal self, with its possibilities of expression in the life of mankind.

Faster and faster the son of God is becoming
aware of his unlimited inheritance. With his understanding has come a quickening of his power. His
rebirth has launched him in a new world, a world
of intelligent substance of which he is the ruler.
He finds his way across and around, above and
underneath both land and sea. He annihilates time
and space. He takes vibrations out of the ether
and hears or sees them, as he chooses. He rises
above the earth and peers downward upon its in-
significance, and reaches upward toward its planetary
kindred.

Divine power has granted us the precious and
exceedingly great promise that we may become par-
takers of the divine nature and thus escape from the
corruption that is in the world. For the earnest ex-
pectation of creation waits for the revealing of the
sons of God, the redemption of the body.

The Domain of Mind

MIND IS ACTUALLY a substantial form of energy. It has been spoken of as static, potential energy, while thought is the dynamic force that produces the activity for manifestation. Science has told us that no energy is ever lost. It may be wasted, but not destroyed. It may always be transmuted from one form into another. We know, then, that thought energy is forceful and creative. As man co-operates and co-ordinates his thought with the infinite purpose, he makes of his mind a meeting place for communion with the infinite intelligence that is God. If he does not choose to recognize the supervision of the divine director, he may walk alone. But he will soon find that of himself he can do nothing that is worthy or profitable. According to Paul, he is not even able to think correctly, for his sufficiency in all things is from God. He is intelligent only to the degree that he uses the infinite intelligence of universal Mind, allowing it to flow through him.

Every man is an individualized satellite in the great solar system of Truth, whose center is God. Each man is, to himself, a separate entity, a little universe in which he lives and moves and has his being, a unit in the universal will. The world in which he dwells is his mind, and its active agency is thought. When we speak of his mind we do not mean an exclusive possession. He can no more lay claim to mind than any one of the planets can appropriate the exclusive use of the sun. God is the one Mind, the whirling source from which all lesser mind words have sprung. Although each may function separately and destroy or cultivate its distinctive attributes, it must move in the orbit of Truth, subject to unerring Principle.

The history of man is the story of individualized mind in its upward trend. Mind is really the one active power in the universe, yet to many people it is still incomprehensible and unintelligible. Like all intangible things of Spirit, which are beyond the cognizance of the senses, mind seems vague and inconsequential unless it is captured and housed in some material form. This is why mind and brain have seemed to be synonymous. Yet we know that this is no more true than the idea that life and body mean the same thing. Material man has so long been a stumbling block to his own spiritual progress that nine people out of ten would probably describe a physical appearance when asked for a definition of man.

But scientists are fast shedding light on the subject of matter. They have come to regard a dynamic universe as far more understandable and realistic than one in a static condition. They tell us that there is no state of stagnation anywhere. Matter is not dense, but alive with fluid energy and vibratory force. Infinitesimal units of life are everywhere creating and producing new cosmic substance. What is the cause that lies back of all this? Something corresponding to an electric force is there, but what keeps it constructive instead of destructive? We fail to understand this until we have the key that unlocks the mystery.

Lately there passed from this plane of existence one who may be termed, in a literal, material sense, the light of the world, just as Jesus may be termed its spiritual prototype. There is no irreverence in this comparison; for certainly Thomas Alva Edison unharnessed and released from the ether floods of radiance that illuminated the entire world. To this man of science, whose religion has been severely questioned by theologians, we may turn for the solution of our mysterious problem. He believed in the existence of a supreme intelligence pervading the universe. This, he was convinced, was a great universal director of destiny, working throughout all creation. Its channel through man is mind.

From its divine source mind draws intelligence to direct the life cells in the human body. Living cells are too minute for microscopical revelation, but finer still are the entities of soul, and farther beyond the reach of any scientific instrument to discover to the senses. It is the intelligence at work in these infinitesimal but unseen entities of Divine Mind that heals and revives the human body. I was told not long ago that science regards the mind as the only enemy to continuous cellular growth. To me, of course, this refers to the human mind, which builds barriers between life and its directing source. The impulse of divine intelligence is to keep life eternal.

We have positive proofs of its untiring efforts in that direction. If the human mind would but co-operate with its source!

In visiting the streets of ancient Pompeii, I marveled at the revelations of modern excavation. It was thrilling to let my imagination travel back over the centuries and see, in fancy, the first Christian heralds relating the wonders of the Nazarene there in the Strada dell' Abbondanza (Street of Abundance). It is related that Paul himself may have walked here, during some of his missionary journeys throughout and beyond the Roman Empire. I seemed to hear this brilliant, scholarly Apostle of the Gentiles telling the story of the Master and the new doctrine to those whose ears were dull and whose eyes were closed to the enlightenment that he was bringing them. They preferred to believe in the solid reality of their substantial stonework; in the things that they could see and hear and touch; in the greatness of Rome and its mighty power. He offered them the light of understanding, but they had darkened their minds with material shadows, preferring to walk by sight rather than by faith; choosing the things that are temporal instead of those that are eternal. And here lay the solid stones they had chosen as realities—poor ghosts of an ancient civilization; shadowy symbols of the fate of tangible reality. The Street of Abundance, the glory that was Rome; where are they now? And how real those unseen, intangible things have become! How solidly dependable, now that the world has come to feel and to recognize the pervading, penetrating spiritual force of Christianity.

Every age repeats, within certain limits, the history of the race. Yet to every age is added experiences that raise the standard of the race. Every man is born into a possession of Truth and knowledge that existed before him and with the opportunity of advancing not only himself, but his age. For each person is born equipped with a great causal agent in the realm of matter. He has the gift of mind, and mind, Professor Pupin says, is the domain of the "creative co-ordinator." This is only another name for what Edison called supreme intelligence. Man may employ this force constructively, or he may use it in building a defensive wall against the entrance of that which he has made his enemy. Whether he stands upon the summit of some spiritual peak and focuses every ray of light upon his life purpose, or whether he burrows into the lowest depths of materiality and seeks to blot out the light of Spirit, Truth continues to shine.

The best thinkers have arrived at the conclusion that Mind in the absolute is perfect. In the individual it is, oftener than not, misused and misapplied, thereby creating imperfect, unpleasant conditions. When these confront him he has an aggrieved feeling that life is to blame; that he has been unjustly dealt with; that he is a puppet of fate; or that God is punishing him for some sinful action.

None of these explanations is true. They are not even sensible reasons. Your mind is your world.

It is your own world. You are its chief executive, responsible for its form of government. As you interpret universal law and enforce it in the thoughts you send out, you make your universe either harmonious or discordant. You must understand that you are free to do as you like, in a sense; but only in the sense of being a viceroy, ruling with viceroyal authority and not with imperial sovereignty. You cannot maintain an autocratic government. You are always responsible to a higher power for the world that has been entrusted to your care. As a ruler you are willing enough to shift your responsibility in times of stress and trial, or to quarrel with the law when it has interfered with your human desires. But to accept gracefully the results of your own mistakes— that is where you have failed, as most of us do.

Manifestations of ill health and inharmonious conditions have to be recognized as such and dealt with accordingly. Abuse or repression will not correct them. Regretful tears will not erase them. They must be traced back to mental states that produced them, and there they must be transmuted or recast in different molds. For back of all material manifestation stands active, living thought. Body and affairs are but passive instruments of mind. They have been created by dynamic thought. If this thought has not been harmonious with the idea in Divine Mind, creation has been untrue and its result is discordant.

When we say that our mind is our world we do not mean to deny the existence of a material world or a material body in which we function, but only its independent existence. They live perpetually in the mind, and we are formed by the image-making faculty of the soul. As Divine Mind projects itself outward into a resultant universe, so we shape and carve our individualized universe out of mind material. The body is an outgrowth of the soul—an effect, of which mind is the cause. It can be reduced back to its essence in Spirit. If we believe it to be material and that it functions in the manner of all flesh, it will not disappoint us. It is created and governed by our own consciousness of it, just as we have visualized it in mind.

The principle of manifestation becomes simple as we come to know and really understand it. It is the scientific law on which all spiritual healing is based. Mind is the reality and the body is its appearance. The body is spirit formulated. Not only is the body subject to this law, but one's life is conditioned by it. We manifest realities in direct ratio to our ideals. That which we hold in mind is bound to be loosed in thought activity and thus objectify itself in form.

In our study of the mind we can scarcely proceed without taking into account two important factors in its development. They are the imagination and the will. Each has been exalted and called the more essential. We remember that Coué insisted that the imaging faculty ranked first as a healing agent. We cannot deny its significance either in healing physical ailments or in changing conditions of living. We know the danger of dwelling upon mental images of failure or poverty, but do we realize the necessity of putting others in place of those that we know must be erased from the consciousness?

I am reminded very forcibly of the remarkable instance of Nijinsky, a once famous young Russian dancer. On his last visit to America, he was the bright particular star of the Diaghileff Ballet Russe, and famous throughout the world. At the outbreak of the war he happened to be in Budapest and became a technical prisoner of the Central Powers. He was allowed, however, to visit America and later to live in Switzerland. As he had no opportunity there for expression through dancing, he turned to painting and drawing, which he had occasionally done in sketching out and devising his dances. At first his subjects were figures—of his little daughter and of his servants. But gradually his mental images changed. He drew haunted faces with staring eyes, and he portrayed over and over again the lines of a soldier's helmet. Finally he painted only dark spaces. He then entered a sanitarium in Switzerland where he spent his time idly dreaming, turning only occasionally to his painting materials. The case is a pertinent illustration of the result of letting an image of frustration gain supremacy in the mind.

On the other hand, there is the memory of a very different case, that of the eminent pianist Vladimir Horowitz. I am always impressed with the psychological significance of a picture of Liszt that Horowitz insists on having in his dressing room on concert nights. Others may call this superstition, but to me it clearly illustrates the idea of a mental image. For of course it is not just a picture, but a representation of something, to the mind of the artist. It suggests genius and sublime attainment.

Every man's mind imprints images of achievement upon his consciousness. These are like seeds, holding within themselves infinite possibilities of development, growth, and fruition. Like seeds, they may represent varied species, each of which will produce its own kind. Two men may image success or money quite clearly, and one will gain high position and enormous wealth. The other will also succeed, but his attainments will be mediocre. Why? One has done his imaging in dimes and dollars, the other in thousands and millions. One has had a vision of getting ahead, while the other has seen himself scaling the heights. These men have proclaimed, through their thought, the restricted or unlimited use that they have made of the divine urge that is ever back of what we call our human mind. This eternal force from within is a divine dissatisfaction compelling us to greater and better effort. It demands perfected images, higher ideals, more powerful thoughts for the manifestation that God would make in our lives.

There are times of revolution in the most efficiently organized country; times when many of its citizens rebel and refuse their allegiance to law and order; times when aliens enter its borders. The government is not responsible for such outbreaks, but *you aren't responsible for birds in the air flying over but, stop them from nesting!*

it is accountable for the havoc produced by continued insubordination. The offenders must be dealt with. In the country or world of your mind you have much the same thing to meet. You are not held accountable for alien thoughts that come in the guise of race beliefs; for fearful thoughts that run riot; for rebellious ideas that seek to overthrow your form of government. But you are entirely responsible for sheltering such enemies or encouraging them to stay with you.

You have as one of your principal executives a powerful agent for enforcement. It has been exalted as highly as its companion power, the imagination. We call it the will, and we know that it can say to this thought "Go!" and to that one "Stay!" just as our mental I chooses. Purposeless, unprofitable aliens must be deported, sent back to the land that gave them birth. Riotous fear must be calmed and quieted by a harmonizing faith. Rebels that refuse allegiance must be dealt with as such—corrected and controlled.

In the world of your mind you must have discipline and this is what the will accomplishes for you. You must have a settled purpose and a steadfast resolution to work toward it. Wisdom and understanding must be yours to employ, not to entertain as idle guests. Every sane person has some degree of understanding. Every sane person is wise in certain directions. Every sane person knows what he ought to do, and very often he feels that he knows exactly what his friends and contemporaries ought to do. But when he is called on to act according to his judgment, he fails without the co-operation of his executive agent, the will.

We must come to think of these two agents of the mind, the imagination and the will, as inseparable. They may work apart, but thus they can accomplish nothing of any worth. In fact each alone may cause havoc in our world. An unrestrained imagination threatens our mental stronghold. A determined will with no purpose is futile. When they join forces and work side by side, our world will be harmonious.

I would not have you misunderstand me by thinking that these are independent powers, or that what we call the human imagination and the human will can successfully work together for ideal accomplishment. They are your agents in your world, and you are responsible to a higher power for their citizenship. They depend on you as you depend on it. You work through them as it works through you. The divine intelligence of universal Mind flows through you as you open yourself to it. Your world is safe only as long as it remains in the orbit of Truth. The sun responds to the earth's need for light and warmth and life. Divine intelligence responds in a far greater measure to your need for sustenance. It is always there and always ready to think and express itself through you.

There is but one Mind, and it is perfect. It knows only what is true. It will enter and possess your consciousness if you will let it. Take your little, human self out of the way and "have this mind in you, which was also in Christ Jesus." That Mind reproduced its knowledge of perfection in many miraculous ways. It refused to recognize any appearance of error. It had no realization of death. That Mind is yours, it is yours now. Let it fill you with the warmth and light of its life, its love, and its Truth.

The Problem of Evil

WHEN AN INTELLECT like George Bernard Shaw feels that the existence of evil is a stumbling block to any belief in a God of perfection, the subject seems to become more than ever a puzzling enigma. It has always been a problem that the human mind found difficult to solve. Very naturally the student's first question is this: "If there is but one presence and power in the universe, that of good, how can evil exist?" Or this: "If God is the infinite Creator, perfect and all good, how did imperfection and chaos come into being? If God is love, and God is all, how do you account for hatred, strife, and war?"

Evil seems to challenge the very omnipotence, omniscience, and omnipresence of God, for how can an all-powerful, all-knowing, ever-present Deity countenance what His supreme intelligence must recognize as entirely antagonistic to all that is good and true? These questions are not alone those of the beginner and the student of Truth, they have aroused bitter controversy among the thinking minds of every age. The answer to all of them must always be that in God's world none of the things we call evil has any existence.

The fact that good and evil, right and wrong, are in continual combat in the world cannot be disputed. We all are only too well aware of this perpetual struggle, and it would be foolish to deny either the presence or the power of evil when its effects are daily brought to our attention. We cannot logically attribute them to the same source, therefore we must seek some explanation that will satisfy the tormenting doubts that so often assail our strongholds of faith.

In judging evil with "righteous judgment" we must look at it from the standpoint of Truth. Truth is the ultimate quest of metaphysics and psychology, of science and religion. The metaphysician, converting all things into their native elements, finds their origin in a fundamental state of being which he terms "infinite reality." He subjects reality to a logical analysis and finds it to be absolute good. His ultimate conclusion is that this reality is the great first cause, and since the cause is good, the effect cannot be otherwise. Considering evil on this basis, it has no existence in reality, hence it is neither principle nor thing but a nonentity, a temporary condition, created by man. It is a manifestation of wrong thinking and has no power except that which is given it in the mind of man. It is a result of ignorance with respect to God, man, and the universe. It has no sustenance of its own, but is a parasite feeding upon human thought and growing great as its victim believes in and fears its power. When that food is withdrawn it dies for lack of nourishment.

The scientist affirms the continuous flow of an infinite stream of energy which harmoniously and intelligently is working forever toward a perfected creation. The energy takes many different forms according to varying rates of vibration. But Truth reveals to the scientist as it does to the metaphysician that all forces—heat, light, electricity, gravitation—are but forms of a universal agent. What the metaphysician terms infinite reality the scientist knows as eternal energy. Atoms and molecules grouped in a divine design result in a faultless organism. Beauty and symmetry of construction are nature's refutation of ugliness and evil, which are manifestations that do not exist in the natural world where divine order is inherent.

Religion leads to the same understanding. With any less than absolute power God would be finite, and such a premise is of course unthinkable. Any normal mind recognizes a God of infinite goodness, free from the dual impulses that sway the human consciousness, an eternal, immutable Creator: both the infinite reality and the eternal energy of the metaphysician and the scientist.

As metaphysics, science, and religion all tell us that evil has no intrinsic existence in either the visible or the invisible universe, our conclusion must be that it is something outside the realm of reality, something perceived and produced only by a chaotic human consciousness and having its origin in a misuse or displacement of that which is inherently good. As it has no existence in Divine Mind, it is in itself a state of negativity, of nothingness, the result of incorrect vision, a chimera of imperfect seeing. It has as much power over us as we ourselves give it by our belief in its actuality.

Man brings about disturbance and destruction through his failure to understand and conform to divine Principle. He departs from Truth and wonders why disorder appears in his life, failing to comprehend that he, through ignorance, has put it in operation. Ignorance does not excuse the culprit in a court of law, neither does it vindicate him at the universal tribunal. His ignorance or deficiency in knowledge of Truth subjects him to inharmonious conditions that affect human life only; no act of his can interfere with the infinite rhythm and heavenly order of divine creation.

Man's belief in evil makes him subject to it and to the death thought that it implies in contradistinction from the God thought that is life. For his own protection he must discover and obey Truth. Ignorance is a negative word, denoting something that is not; it suggests lack. Evil as ignorance signifies a deficiency in the knowledge of Truth in human consciousness. Sickness and disease indicate lack of wholeness; poverty and limitation are lack of supply; inharmony and unhappiness are the results of lack of good.

War, poverty, disease, and death are the great enemies of mankind. They will never be abolished until we overcome the conditions that give them power over us. Peace can never dominate war until individuals cease hating one another, and jealousy, criticism, condemnation, and intolerance no longer exist. All the troubles that come upon us are the effect of "seeing double" instead of seeing with the "single eye" of wisdom. Our belief in duality recognizes the existence of two powers, good and evil; of two substances, spirit and matter.

In the allegorical narrative of the temptation and fall of man the serpent represents the sensuous appearance reported by an imperfect sense perception. This imperfection was not a unique experience of one man, Adam, but is a daily occurrence in each life. We repeat the fall of man every time we accept the false testimony of materiality and allow it to control and dominate us. Through the perception of Truth we rise again to walk in newness of life, through clarity of understanding.

"Ye shall know the truth, and the truth shall make you free" was the principle of the Master, who made Truth the supreme objective of Christianity. There never was a greater scientist or metaphysician than Jesus, and He recognized a perfect, spiritual realm in which no flaw of evil existed. "Which of you convicteth me of sin?" He asked. He dwelt in a spiritual realm, a kingdom of heaven, where no man could convince Him of the reality of evil or sin. His ability to "take away" or forgive the sins of the world lay in His clarity of vision. He understood them to be the result of thinking outside the principles of Divine Mind and failing to measure up to Truth. We, too, may forgive the sins of the race by refusing to judge by appearance, exercising righteous judgment instead; by recognizing man as an infinite idea of an infinite mind and refusing to stamp his mistakes upon his consciousness.

Sense perception has been corrected many times during the history of mankind. It once believed the earth to be flat and to be the center of the solar system; it looked upon electricity as a destructive power of the elements; it ridiculed the idea that anything heavier than air could rise above the earth. What man calls his common sense once told him that all these absurd appearances were true. But these and many other beliefs are now utterly absurd in the illumination of truth. Columbus proved that the earth is round, Copernicus that the sun has a central position, Franklin that electricity could become man's slave, the Wright brothers that humanity could become air-minded. Jesus established the greatest of all truths, namely that man is not material and destructible but a spiritual being whom death cannot annihilate.

Spiritual illumination corrects all misconceptions of the sense man and reveals the true design of man's life and work. This is attained only by correct thinking based upon the principles of eternal reality. A principle is a truth that, when understood and applied, reveals the original reality. False thinking is failure to apply the principle, either through ignorance or willfulness. Its remedy is re-education accomplished through desire to learn or induced by means of disciplinary effects brought about by that which we call evil.

Just as we become hopelessly entangled in a mathematical problem when we fail to work with the rule, so we plunge our life into confusion when we think and act in opposition to spiritual principle. The incorrect result we obtain we call evil, and by fearing or resisting it we recognize its influence, which only strengthens it and amplifies its power over us. Battling against it can never defeat it. There is only one solvent and that is Truth. One does not fight with the wrong solution of a mathematical problem; one erases one's figures and carefully proceeds once more, paying greater attention to the principle involved. The absolute knowledge that the principle is sound, whether correctly applied or not, gives a calm conviction of success.

Every time we think or act against Truth we fall short of the mark of our high calling, and this we understand to be sin. Sin produces disastrous results, as it is the nature of every thought to become manifest. These results are distressing to the thinker, who gives them power by believing in their reality. Actually they have no archetype in the realm of Spirit, being mere false appearances in a world of sense.

"The way of the transgressor is hard," for in his spiritual blindness he often stumbles and falls, being unable to see clearly through the medium of sense that blurs his visions. His road to destruction is broad but not smooth, as it contains many pitfalls. Many danger signals and detour instructions are posted along his way, warnings of pain, inharmony, and failure—all indications that he is not on the right thoroughfare.

Under the old dispensation we learned a great

deal about a God who punishes sinners. The high-
way to destruction, entered through a wide gate was
pictured as a broad, easy road to thrilling adventure,
but he who chose it was by way of punishment to be
plunged into a fiery furnace in the hereafter. It is
to be hoped that no such teaching is part of any
religious education today. God does not punish sin.
Its consequences are contained within it, just as the
flower is held in the tiny seed, awaiting development.

"Every one that committeth sin is the bond-
servant of sin." He could have no other master than
this, for sin makes exorbitant demands on its slaves,
and the only wages it pays are misery, disease, and
death. Moreover the working conditions provided
by sin are unsatisfactory and unsanitary, and they
grow into a treadmill of negative disintegration.
As sense illusions increase, impaired vision grows
apace and reality is lost in shadowy darkness. Thus
hell is experienced, a sense of separation, the final
objective of evil and sin.

Temptation to sin comes to every person; the
Devil of subconscious race belief in the material
spares no one. Even the Master was required to
meet and subdue him. Jesus was "tempted of the
devil," and His threefold temptation was in each
case an effort of the devil of material belief to triumph over the spiritual reality that was the Master's supreme ideal. These three temptations included every sin that menaces the well-being of man,
and they may be analyzed under the headings of
pride, sensuality, and avarice. Dante's imagination

pictured them in the form of animals: the panther, the lion, and the she-wolf.

The subtle sensual or material subconscious belief urged a use of spiritual power for the gratification of the sense man. "If thou art the Son of God, command that these stones become bread." It was an appeal to the flesh appetite and conveyed discipline of mind. "Man shall not live by bread alone, but by every word that proceedeth out of the mouth of God." As a spiritual being man must raise his body, through his mastery of it, to the level of its spiritual ideal.

Pride is that self-exultation that isolates man from both God and his fellow men. The devil of subconscious beliefs tells him he is entirely independent of any power save his own and thus imprisons him within a sense of separate existence. "Then the devil taketh him into the holy city; and he set him on the pinnacle of the temple, and saith unto him, If thou art the Son of God, cast thyself down: for it is written,

He shall give his angels charge concerning thee: and

On their hands they shall bear thee up,

Lest haply thou dash thy foot against a stone." Power flows through man that he may employ it unselfishly in the service of "the son" or race of mankind. If he falls into the snare of using it selfishly or foolishly for his own greedy achievement, he closes the avenue through which he receives the power. He may not *try* God, he must *prove* Him.

Hence the second admonition: "It is written, Thou shalt not make trial of the Lord thy God."

The third temptation is avarice. What a train of satellites belong to it! What a mountain of false thought man has raised upon it! The "devil" of material possessions is always whispering, "All these things will I give thee, if thou wilt fall down and worship me." The followers of avarice are its constant, energetic agents, ceaselessly tempting and enslaving men. They include jealousy, strife, envy, dishonesty, murder, and countless others. Jesus met this final test positively and decisively: "It is written, Thou shalt worship the Lord thy God, and him only shalt thou serve."

We read that after these temptations angels came and ministered unto Jesus. We understand this to mean that divine ideas took possession of His Spirit and strengthened Him, just as every man is strengthened today through the attainment of self-mastery. Victory over the mortal beliefs that bind him to the earth frees him from all fear of evil and gives him the dominion that is his birthright. He does not find it necessary to strive for place or possessions; he knows that when he seeks first the kingdom, all things are automatically added to his life.

Great works followed Jesus' triumph over materiality. His loyalty to a spiritual ideal glorified His life. It will do the same for you and for me. The same angels of true ideas inspire us today when we steadfastly meet and conquer the tempting allurement of the senses. Each conquest strengthens the real or spiritual nature and augments the faculty that promotes it. Shirking or running away from a problem never solved it. Ignoring a temptation never vanquished it. Every man's enemy must be met face to face in the firm conviction that "greater is he that is in you than he that is in the world." Every man's life may thus become glorified, and he may stand unafraid before his Father and his fellow men. "He that overcometh shall inherit these things."

In Reality, which is the consciousness of God, evil does not exist. It is created by man in wrong thinking (out of line with Principle). Belief in evil makes man subject to it and its consequences of all sickness, inharmony, poverty, etc. Sin is falling short of Reality. We can overcome by saying with Jesus, ①, ②, and ③ included in the chapter.

Spiritual Re-Education

TWO PRELIMINARY STEPS are required of the student who is about to begin his spiritual re-education. Just as a child must learn first things first, beginning with the simplest mathematical principles, so man finds it necessary to school his consciousness in primary, elemental exercises. Of the two steps, denial and affirmation, one is simply a preparator for the other. Denial is the demolisher that clears the mind of dangerous impedimenta and razes obstructions that have been erected by false belief and wrong reasoning; while affirmation is the builder that must follow up the destructive process by substituting that which is real and eternal.

Many hundreds of years before the time of Jesus, the Egyptians used the sign of the cross to indicate a "crossing" or blotting out of evil spirits. It is still employed by the Catholic Church with something of the same significance. Those who knew Mary Baker Eddy personally say that the secret of her great healing power lay in her absolute denial of apparent conditions. "It is not so" was her challenge to every appearance of disease.

The Master spoke often of the efficacy of denial, calling it by various names and explaining it with a wealth of illustration. He called attention to the danger of leaving the inside of the cup uncleansed. He likened it to removing withered and unfruitful branches; to uprooting cumbersome plants; to a grain of wheat giving itself up to the process of growth in order to attain perfection.

Jesus taught the denial of self as a voluntary setting aside of all false beliefs, both those which have come to us by racial inheritance and those which have been reported to us by the material sensations of the natural man—that wretched flesh man whom Paul described as striving and warring with the inner or spiritual man. Who shall deliver us from that body of death? Who indeed but He who by denying their enmity created of these two a new man, a man who "hath been in all points tempted like as *we are, yet* without sin," a man who by establishing peace between these two antagonists abolished "the law of sin and of death."

Man is the result of all that he has thought, but his list of thoughts contains many false items. He must erase his errors and fill in his omissions before he can get a correct result. He must blot the undesirable out of his subconscious mind. Unsound, old mental structures must be torn down and destroyed. His lesser self must "die daily." That is what denial can accomplish for him. It is not something that affects God; it is a re-education that dredges channels for the inflow of Truth. It makes "straight the way of the Lord." It is the ax at the root of the unfruitful tree; the fan that blows away the chaff for the thorough cleansing of the threshing floor. Is your body racked with pain? Is your life darkened by sorrow or inharmony? Are your desires stinted by lack and want? If you are giving attention to these manifestations, they will increase their power over you. Such ugly, distorted conditions may seem real, but they are only the shadows of impedimenta that you carry about with you and that you may discard at will.

As a destructive force denial is very necessary in the erasure of troublesome mental problems, but care should be taken to prevent its excessive use, as it often results in a negative, passive state of consciousness. In mathematical parlance, it would be designated by a minus sign in contradistinction from the plus symbol of the positive. They are significant designations, as they tell the story of lack or lessening, on the one hand, as contrasted with addition or gain, on the other.

When the consciousness has been cleansed of error, the first step has been taken. Unsightly old beliefs have been demolished and removed. First things have been done first. The destruction of the negative conditions not only suggests but necessitates a like process of reconstruction. When old buildings are torn down, the ground is available for new and improved structures. As unstable, mental negations are cleared away, the student may replace them with positive, substantial ideas.

According to the parable, the swept and garnished house of spirit should not be left empty; it must be occupied, against the reappearance of its former inhabitant. This undesirable tenant, failing to find a new home and perhaps not quite convinced of the finality of his eviction, is apt to return to his late dwelling place. Finding it still vacant, and attracted by the clean, unobstructed spaciousness, he may gather together a family of seven companions even more worthless than himself, and in a body they are likely to take possession and dwell there. And so, the moral is pointed, the last state of that house is worse than the first.

Nature cannot endure barren emptiness; she will not allow vacant spaces. Her inclination is to fill in and complete. She covers the uncultivated field with a garment of beauty. She pours fluid streams into dry channels. Nor does she overlook the rocky cliffs and sultry deserts. Each after its kind and according to its environment must bring forth something.

This law of vital productivity in the natural world applies equally to man; therefore he must be on his guard against the reactions of his destructive activities. His sword must be two-edged. As he tears down, he must also rebuild. He must substitute a positive for each discarded negative, always remembering that denial may become a powerful vampire, extracting the very lifeblood of the person who lacks a proper understanding of its use. I once knew a man whose extravagant employment of negation had weakened him almost to the point of dissolution. When this was pointed out to him, he learned ever after to "nerve himself with incessant affirmatives."

Since the body has been so aptly called a house or temple, we may well learn a lesson from the builder. His materials are important, his labor is necessary, but both are useless if he has no blueprint. In our rebuilding of the body temple, our affirmations must not be scattered about aimlessly and formlessly. In order to rear a successful structure we need a perfect design. We need to make all things after the pattern given in the Mount—that original blueprint whose architect and draftsman was God. We must keep this model continually before us, perpetuating it in our consciousness so that it shall not be lost or mislaid even for a moment. Shadows may intervene and interfere with our vision or perhaps entirely obscure it from our view. But we must recognize this as a time of testing. Denial is so much easier than steadfast affirmation. But a mind that has been re-educated in the knowledge of Truth will stand fast, and its very steadfastness is in itself a powerful affirmation.

I know a man at the head of a large trust company who has refused to let the negative shadows of depression and unemployment discourage him. In the midst of the trying conditions of the past few years he has remained steadfastly confident that nothing can thwart the divine plan. That man hasn't a negative in his nature. He does not know the meaning of failure. He continues to demonstrate in his affairs the success that accompanies the positive power behind which lies the force of an affirmative attitude. He is but one of many who possess this plus or positive power and who stand forth boldly and proclaim it. I do not mean that we should shout our convictions from the housetops. Silence is often a more forcible convincer. "What you are . . . thunders so that I cannot hear what you say." The Truth student who goes about antagonizing his family and friends by insistently affirming his opinions about conditions makes a great mistake. Many homes and friendships have been wrecked on the rock of overzealous affirmation.

An outstanding characteristic of Christianity is its positiveness. Its founder was no weakling dealing in negatives. When the afflicted sought His help, He did not say that He would *try* to do something for them; or that *perhaps* their loved ones would be restored to them. When great rulers came to Him for advice, He did not bow fearfully before their age or superiority, or question His ability to counsel them. He spoke as one having authority; "Thou art made whole." "Lazarus, come forth." "Ye must be born anew." He used affirmatives only. There wasn't a negative in Him. There was always the majestic conviction that is the soul of leadership. Difficulties vanished in the blaze of His assurance.

To that father whose very human appeal was, "If thou canst do anything, have compassion on us, and help us," His reply was a lesson in the use of affirmatives. *If* He could! How long must He bear with their futile, negative doubting? "If thou canst!" He repeated. "All things are possible to him that believeth." To the student who asks what good is to be gained by saying something one doesn't believe, I would answer, "Keep on repeating the

words. Affirm them often enough and the healing
of your unbelief will follow." There is something
so powerful in the sound of emphatic affirmation
that it overcomes all human reasoning. We often
say that people "bluff," which means, of course, that
they have succumbed to the affirmative repetition of
some seeming impossibility.

So many of us are uncertain, indecisive, fearful.
We go through life divided against ourselves mentally. Jesus came with a distinct mission—that of
fulfillment: to rebuild instead of to tear down; to
conserve, not dissipate, power. He had listened to
the thundering denunciations of John the Baptist
calling the people to repent. He realized the necessity of following up this cleansing process with
something effective, something positive. What John
emptied, He must fill; where John had denounced
and torn down, He must rebuild. What John had
prepared, He must organize for active service.

"I came not to destroy, but to fulfill." He demonstrated the truth of these words in all His relationships. He did not criticize His followers' lack
of education or belittle their humble calling. With
the mighty affirmative force of His being He set
about the task of re-educating them spiritually. "I
will make you fishers of men," He assured them.
He fulfilled this promise so truly that all who came
in touch with them "took knowledge of them, that
they had been with Jesus." He molded them into
superior writers and teachers because of His extraordinary power of recognizing their hidden ca-

pacities and because of His positive faith in His own ability to develop them. "We have the mind of Christ" was their proud affirmation.

We shall never be able to manifest perfection with an imperfect model before us. How can we expect to build after the divine plan of our birth-right of health if we are continually refusing to see the pattern of wholeness? Are we, perhaps, always affirming negatives? There is no surer way to ill health than eternally declaring that we are not well. There is no shorter route to the poorhouse than the "can't-afford-it" habit of limitation. There is no easier way to be miserable than by the self-pity that recognizes lack everywhere in our lives.

"Thou shalt also decree a thing, and it shall be established unto thee." Does this mean nothing to us? When we decree pain, old age, and death for the body, how can we expect the health, the youth, and the life we so earnestly desire? To decree lack and failure is to establish them in our affairs. In decreeing inharmony and discontent, we ordain them in our consciousness. We may establish the pattern of health in our body and fail to recognize supply as our divine inheritance. Or we may decree substance for ourselves and miss the spirit of good will. Why do we not claim our heritage in its entirety? Why not decree our sonship, therefore our rightful heir-ship to "all things whatsoever the Father hath?"

Job suffered long and grievously before he realized that he had been utterly mistaken in his understanding of God. "I will demand of thee, and

declare thou unto me," he said at last. We, too, have
heard many misinterpretations of God, and we have
heard Him blamed for self-imposed wretchedness of
mind and body. We have heard the unenlightened
argue and moan and implore, and all the time we
have known that they were uttering that which they
did not understand.

"I will demand of thee." Shall we not thus un-
lock the inner treasure vault and draw upon its hidden resources? Let us open our eyes of faith and
behold our divine birthright. Let us substitute affirmatives for negatives and see that which is, instead
of that which is not. We can put visions of success
and achievement in place of failure and despair.
We can demand our perfection—of health, of joy, of
supply. Let us daily affirm these, silently and steadfastly, and construct, according to the pattern of the
Mount, our house of positive being.

Let us "be still, and know" that our Redeemer
liveth, that He is God, and that "in quietness and in
confidence" shall be our strength. Let us be persuaded that "neither death, nor life, nor angels, nor
principalities, nor things present, nor things to come,
nor powers, nor height, nor depth, nor any other
creature, shall be able to separate us from the love
of God." "For I know him whom I have believed,
and I am persuaded that he is able to guard that
which I have committed unto him." This is our
confident "assurance of *things* hoped for," our positive "conviction of things not seen."

Efficacious Prayer

effective

M AN HAS ALWAYS prayed and he always will; it is his nature to seek the Source of his being. There is a time in every person's life when he feels the need of a power greater than his own. In such moments the human spirit, yearning for strength and guidance, reaches out after something and sends forth its appeal as naturally as a child turns to its parents for help.

As man recognizes his own weakness and his inability to satisfy his longings and attain his ideals, he instinctively acknowledges his dependence upon a wisdom and a force beyond his little human ability. Prayer is both the "soul's sincere desire" and its recognition of its innately divine origin as well as the means whereby it obtains its sustenance. However we choose to look at it—as nature, destiny, evolution, or God—the power of prayer is the great basic activity that pervades the mystery of life.

Every thinking person must feel that his life is both derived and dependent. Correctly interpreted, it is a valuable trust fund placed in his charge, which he is to preserve, control, and account for. Man and his sustenance are inseparable and interdependent, man being as essential to the expression of his Creator as the Creator is to the existence of His creation.

Man can do nothing of himself. His very handiwork is imitative rather than creative. In re-creating the wonders of nature he reproduces its harmony as music, its forms as sculpture; he paints its beauties in rainbow hues, and calls his reproductions "works of art." His inventions reflect the influence of the creations of the natural world: he imitates the creatures of the sea and produces great ocean liners. From the birds of the air he conceives the idea of taking unto himself wings and flying to "the uttermost part of the earth." Whatever he does seems an acknowledgment that his life and his work proceed from a source deeper and more powerful than anything that he can clearly explain.

It is a pointed reminder that man's being is rooted in a life greater than that of his individual existence. He is a sublime exposition and expression of the mighty fountain of vitality, ever bubbling from the heart of creation. Within him he carries a memory of his origin, an ever-increasing urge to seek and to discern its true meaning. Whatever he may call this consuming desire to comprehend and appropriate his good, this sincere longing of his soul for satisfaction, it is in reality a form of prayer. Only the Creator of the universe can satisfy his needs, therefore his life is incomplete without prayer.

Prayer has evolved and progressed with the growth of human understanding. It has kept pace with man's conscious intelligence and has been a silent witness to the actuality of his divine kinship. Primitive man, dominated by fear, made his appeal to what seemed the controlling power in his environment. He paid homage to the sun and stars, to fire and water, to animals and plants, and to images and myths. As his intellect developed it demanded something more responsive than nature and her elemental forces. His human ideas conceived a personal Deity and invested it with his own sentiments and characteristic emotions.

The anthropomorphic God of the early Hebrews with His human traits and physical sensibilities was the natural inference of a groping intellect searching for some tangible means of augmenting its development. We read in our Scriptures of the first conversations with this personal Deity and of the baleful effect of fear, which kept His worshipers from intimate contact and friendly association with the true source of their being. This fear, among the Hebrews as elsewhere, originated in a sense of guilt, a realization of man's disobedience to law. It led man into devious paths of ignorance and error, arousing in him the idea that he must implore forgiveness, and developing in him a demoralizing "worm-of-the-dust" consciousness.

As man grew gradually to recognize the power of earthly rulers, he came to attribute the same sovereignty to his God, investing Him with the authority to punish and avenge at will, and looking upon Him as a being to be appeased by sacrificial offerings and assailed with pleas for favor. He approached Him timidly and fearfully, with a recital of the worthy and unworthy actions of His suppliant. He implored Him to withhold His displeasure and to bestow His blessings. Very often he instructed Him just why and how He should provide the desired benefits. He, the finite, besieged the Infinite and entreated Him to distribute His largess in favor of those whose appeals were most emphatic and whose arguments were most convincing.

However much prayer has been misunderstood and misapplied, it is woven into the very fabric of human life. There are prayers that have been efficacious and prayers that have not, just as there are people who pray with understanding and those who do not. All men in all ages and all races have prayed in one way or another. Although the list of unanswered prayers may be long, yet in the history of prayer we read the history of religion, we might almost say the history of humanity. The elevation from its crude origin to finer forms reveals a spiritual and intellectual advance and proclaims an upward progress in man's evolutionary journey.

Wisdom has brought great changes in our interpretation of God, and understanding has defined prayer in modern terms. We have come to apprehend Him as living principle rather than as a quasi-human personality. After thousands of years of searching, we have found Him in mind and have learned to know Him, through His attributes, as the ever-present, all-powerful activity of Spirit. We have discerned that He is seeking to bestow His infinite goodness on man and thus to accomplish the ultimate of creation. This conclusion reveals prayer as the direct line of communication between man and the power that created him and sustains him, providing a complete supply for his every need in the universal kingdom of the absolute. The connection can never be outgrown or broken off, for through it man receives life into his consciousness. It is a transfusion of infinite strength and power from the great reservoir of supply to the weakened, failing spirit of human endeavor.

Each individual is an outlet and an agent for the unlimited resources of Spirit. God is the divine capacity to give, man the receptive agency of expression. To the degree that man puts himself at the disposal of the universal as an outlet for spiritual energy, he utilizes its forces and brings into manifestation its quickening power. If in his ignorance he requires understanding; if he is sick, unhappy, or poor beyond the endurance of his little personal self, the Father principle is waiting with infinite wealth of resources to make good the deficit, whatever it may be. The only requirement is agreement or cooperation on the part of the needy one. He must remove his lesser self, which proves a barrier between himself and God.

The Hebrew word translated in our English Bible as "pray" or "prayer" is derived from a root word, *palal,* that has various forms. Its signification lends wonderful meaning to its English derivative. In its essence it denotes "judging oneself to be marvelously made," "recognizing wondrous things within the self continually and habitually." Where is the person who has fully recognized this high spiritual import of prayer? Who remembers to recognize himself as a wondrous miracle made in God's image, and to do this "continually and habitually."

According to the ancient Hebrew word the human spirit, in its instinctive search for some reality to satisfy its longings and to objectify its ideals, must receive its reply from within. Its prayer is like a wire that carries to the outer life a current of energy from an inner powerhouse in whose batteries is stored the dynamic consciousness of God. To contact this consciousness is to practice the presence of God.

True prayer realizes the orderly, harmonious creation of Spirit; it thinks in terms of reality and rises into the perfection of Divine Mind. True prayer means coming into the light of Truth through correct insight into Being. True prayer brings about the demonstration of divine law by applying and appropriating the infinite goodness according to spiritual principle. True prayer helps us to appreciate the beauty and the wonders of the world in which we live; it comforts us with a companionship that cannot be taken away; it renews our courage, enlarges our blessings, and disciplines us in the school of service. It is that light in which we "shall . . . see light."

We pray in order that the divine will may be done in and through us. If harmony is lacking in our human affairs, prayer will bring it into manifestation, for prayer is divine adjustment. But the adjustment cannot be made over a barrier of disagreement. Consider the advice of Jesus: "If therefore thou art offering thy gift at the altar, and there rememberest that thy brother hath aught against thee . . . first be reconciled to thy brother, and then come and offer thy gift." Human adjustment must be made to the full extent of human understanding before spiritual exercise can be effective: the barrier between man and man remains also a barrier between man and God. Agreement with all creation and its eternal completion is the law of prayer. Only as man lives in harmony with Divine Mind are all things possible to him. He must rise out of the imperfect beliefs of the race and come into direct alignment with the original thought of his Creator. His failure to do this results in the ills and sorrows of the world. "For with thee is the fountain of life"; and any interference with its spontaneous, free-flowing activity inhibits its stream of vital, life-sustaining nourishment.

Conformation to principle banishes all bondage to sense. Just as vivid sunlight banishes fearful night shadows, so the intense radiance of Truth exposes the impotence of materiality and its adversities. Living in the consciousness of the human outlook has dwarfed man's ability to see clearly. Only in his application of divine principle through prayer lies his remedy for lack, ignorance, and misery. Prayer is "a very present help in trouble" and should be as spontaneous a movement of spiritual instinct as is reflex action of the muscles to physical stimulus.

To Jesus prayer was nothing unique or spasmodic; it was as much a part of Him as breathing or thinking. In our record of His daily life we find Him constantly withdrawing from the crowds in

order to renew His strength by spiritual transfusion.
He stressed the necessity of our becoming as little
children before we can enter the kingdom of heaven
or harmony. We must become as receptive mentally
as the little child if we are to learn to pray effectually.
In studying the science of prayer we must master
certain spiritual principles, just as the young child
begins by mastering the alphabet or learns how to
apply the rules of arithmetic in adding up a column
of figures. Before a scientific principle can be fully
demonstrated it must be understood, and prayer is
a science involving accurate agreement with law just
as truly as mathematics or music.

Truth students know that Truth is valid and that
the correct solution to a problem is the result of
work according to the laws of Truth. Yet people
are continually complaining that their prayers are
never answered. A suggestion that possibly they do
not know how to pray arouses their indignation. To
those who followed Jesus—His close friends and
disciples—prayer was very likely a daily experience,
yet one of them said, "Lord, teach us to pray."

Like all of us, the disciples probably thought
they knew how to pray. But when they noted how
the Master's prayers were always answered and their
own were not, it is no wonder they attributed His
success to some secret prayer formula as yet un-
known to them; hence their very humble request for
instruction. Yet Jesus taught prayer quite simply;
not as a mysterious incantation but as a spiritual exercise. He spoke often of the manner of its accom-

plishment. The lengthy, public, recitative devotions
of the Pharisees so offended His sensitive spirit that
He advised His disciples to pray not for effect, standing in public places to "be seen of men," nor by the
use of "vain repetitions," thinking to be heard "for
their much speaking." He taught them to enter into
the quiet, secret place of the individual spirit and,
closing the door against all intrusion, to commune
there silently with the Father; to "ask . . . believing," and to forgive: "Pray for them that persecute
you."

It has taken man a long time to grasp the Master's advice with respect to approaching the Infinite:
"Enter into thine inner chamber, and having shut
thy door, pray to thy Father who is in secret, and thy
Father who seeth in secret shall recompense thee."
For thousands of years man has sought something
in the "without," when all the time his "city of
refuge" has been within himself. "To recognize
wondrous things within the self!" Jesus was but
stating this idea in metaphor when He spoke of entering into the "inner chamber." To Him this was
penetrating the place of perfect thought, the treasure
vault where wondrous things are stored beyond the
hazard of moth, rust, and thief. It means entering
the presence of the "one God and Father of all, who
is over all, and through all, and in all."

"And having shut thy door." Having entered
the place of illumination, you must shut out all
thought of self. As the ancient Jehovah required
Moses to come up into the mount alone for the re-

ception of the law, so each soul must approach its Sinai of communion alone. The door must close out all turmoil of race thoughts, all delusions of material belief, and the clamorous demands of sense.

"Pray to thy Father who is in secret." In the hidden recesses of your own soul, you will find wondrous things—the courage, the inspiration, and the joy you are seeking. There, in the place of adjustment, you will discover the magic mirror in which the true self is reflected as the image and likeness of the Creator.

"And thy Father who seeth in secret shall recompense thee." Not alone in the secret place, but openly, will the answer be received. As Moses' face shone by reason of his communion with Jehovah long after he had come down from His presence, so we shall carry with us into the outer the shining adjustment of Spirit that we have received. The reward is a natural result, an expression of the perfection we have beheld and of the wondrous possibilities within ourselves.

No semblance of prayer can lift us above self-consciousness and show us the true reality we find in a realization of our Father. The servile, antiquated beseechings for mercy, the pleading and begging for favors, are all proofs of our lack of understanding. They regard the Father as a human deity, possessing even less force of character and determination of will than many human beings manifest. To suppose that wailing and entreating may change an entire omnipotent plan just to please or accommodate one human demand is, to say the least, an attitude of arrogant presumption.

The universe is governed by unfailing law. Nothing is accidental. Nothing "just happens." Back of every effect is a specific cause. If universal law were not dependable, we could expect the cosmos to be reduced to chaos at any moment. Since prayer has been answered not once but many times, we are reasonably certain that it is subject to definite, unfailing laws that if properly complied with will produce a desired result. This result will not be a favor that is granted by some being who gives or withholds at his discretion; it will be an inevitable outworking of immutable principle.

In thus treating prayer as a science subject to universal law we are compelled to discard much of what we have been taught about God and religion in general. We are fast learning to know God as living activity, creative force, infinite Spirit. Although many are still seeing "in a mirror, darkly," we know that spiritual sight grows ever clearer, and the day is fast approaching when all shall see "face to face."

This scientific age has transformed a static universe into a fluid, vibrating one, and has utilized the energy of that fluidity in the service of mankind. It should follow, quite logically, that man may advance toward the rediscovery of prayer as strong, spiritual energy. More and more the world is recognizing thought as a powerful force subject to certain fixed laws and capable of being applied and directed.

Intense desire in the human soul is a prayer energy that uses thought as its operating medium, and the response or reaction to this energy, when applied in accordance with law, is no more mysterious than the effect of any other applied principle. The physicist measuring sound and light vibrations under certain proved conditions achieves definite results. The chemist, the astronomer, and the musician each applies a working principle, and each gets an answer. But with this dynamic, potent energy of Spirit, this prayer force, man has accomplished little because he has not regarded prayer as a science requiring the fulfillment of certain necessary conditions.

When our prayers are not answered, we cannot understand that we and not God are to blame for the failure. Spiritual thinking is powerful, but it must be reinforced by clear vision, deep desire, strong faith, and patient, sustained effort. We cannot expect desire alone to bring results. Few of us have a definite, vivid picture of our ideal or much faith in its manifestation, and rarely are we willing to "pray without ceasing."

Prayer energy is fashioned within the quiet laboratory of the soul. Attuned to the vibration of faith and sustained by persistent contact with its vital battery of Spirit, this force is broadcast to every station of man's being, until all its relationships become expressions of prayer. In accordance with the law of action and reaction, it rebounds or "expresses itself" in exact proportion to the strength of the original stimulus. It has the polarity of any force: the negativity that is receptive or subjective, and the positivity that is manifest in the objective.

Efficacious prayer is the result of making contact with the consciousness of God. This consciousness cannot be approached over barriers of poor, sick, unhappy beliefs. There is no room in the laboratory of the "inner chamber" for burdens and problems. Only true and perfect ideas may enter here, where we must recognize God in the wondrous things within the self, and receive the inspiration of Spirit, before we can project it into our affairs.

The student of Truth knows he cannot ask for anything that God has not already provided. He knows himself to be an outlet for ultimate perfection. His prayer, then, will never be a plea for more, but a petition to see what already is, and thereafter continually and habitually to recognize that vision of reality until it becomes manifest as the concrete result of its own energy.

Faith Is Effective

FAITH IS A KIND OF KNOWLEDGE based on trust; a positive belief in what we judge to be true. It is not a state or activity of any particular mental faculty, but rather a combined activity of the entire personality. It is expectant and prophetic; adventurous, courageous, creative. It is both a discoverer and a builder. It aspires and inspires. It is half vision and half power to express that vision. Really to believe is to have, for faith is the assurance of things hoped for, and the conviction that unseen things must become tangible. It gives us the ability to advance fearlessly into the possibilities of the realm of Spirit and to believe them into visibility.

We are constantly being reminded that the great need of today is a revival of faith. Just what is meant is not always clear, as the general public is confused about its meaning and skeptical regarding its practical value. To the fundamentalist, faith suggests religion only. It means belief in certain forms of worship as set forth in creed and dogma. It is what theology preaches as a means of salvation: faith in the literal truth of ancient propositions and outworn rituals. A revival of faith, from this point of view, must be a return of religious zest, inspired by a resumption of long-established church doctrine.

The modern scientist, who believes only in intellectual propositions, is hostile to the theologian's point of view. To him, a revival of such faith would mean a return to ancient, ignorant superstition. He offers what is, to him, positive proof that religious faith should be relegated to the Dark Ages, and he makes a formal declaration of war on behalf of his up-to-date knowledge against the fundamentalist's lack of modernism.

But there is another class that calls itself modern and that includes many of our most scientific intellects. These do not recognize any hostility between science and true religion. But they do not confuse religious faith with theological doctrine. They know that science is still confronted with many mysterious secrets and that he who would discover them must walk by faith, not by sight. The kind of faith we need to revive today is not that which contradicts science, nor that which is overwhelmed by it, but rather the faith that co-operates with it; the faith that recognizes scientific achievement as the "works" without which faith is without use or profit.

Strange as it may seem, we find the best, most comprehensive meaning of faith in the works of a brilliant letter writer of ancient times. No more remarkable understanding of the word exists than that written many years ago by Paul to the Hebrews. His definition of it has nothing to do with religious creed; it does not concern itself with supposition or belief. It is substantial, dealing with the substance of Spirit and the tangible evidence into which unseen things may be shaped. It does not stop with the vision, but includes that which should follow, the demonstration, or "works."

This extraordinary letter contains the most marvelous chapter about faith accomplishment that has ever been compiled. Yet we could equal if not surpass it today by a record of twentieth-century creations of faith. Time would certainly fail us to tell, in one short chapter, of Burbank, and Edison, of Curtiss and the Wright brothers, of Lindbergh and Byrd and Earhart, of Einstein and Eddington, of Pupin, Jacks, and Millikan, and numberless others who compose the cloud of witnesses by which our modern life is encompassed; and of how, through their faith, natural forces have been subdued, conquered, and placed under man's dominion. Faith in the unseen reality has literally removed mountains of earth and cast them into the sea; it has quickened human sight and hearing; it has annihilated time and space; it has given men eagle's wings and made them air-minded instead of earthbound. All scientific demonstration is the result of faith—light, heat, locomotion, even our food, containing, as it does, the faith of the planter in a law of growth and fruition.

We walk by faith in many ways, every day of our lives. In fact, we can scarcely take a step in any direction that does not imply confidence in some person or thing or principle. We may not always call it faith, but it rules us even when we are largely unconscious of its presence and power. We speak of proving a principle, but our belief does not wait on the proof; we seek to prove it because we first believe in it. Proof follows belief.

There is nothing static or stagnant about faith. It is always an active quality involving thought, feeling, and will. It combines these with the adventurous courage that steps forth boldly on its quest. Faith is the first requisite to success, but "what does it profit, my brethren, if a man say he hath faith, but have not works? can that faith save him?" James goes on to tell us that "faith, if it have not works, is dead," just as the body without the spirit has no life. We often speak of a living faith. In reality there is no other kind. Faith is a dynamic force calling for active application.

It is quite true that the world today is passing through a period of what seems like a loss of faith in many things. Honesty, justice, good will, safety —all these appear very often to be tottering on their foundations. But we know that this is only a lethargic condition. The faith of the world can and will be revived. It is not a time for glossing over conditions with pious platitudes. The world is floundering in a bog of problems that cannot be met with mere optimism. We all are feeling, more or less, the pressure of the struggle of men to disentangle themselves from the conditions of discouragement and despondency into which they have fallen. If we have escaped a direct effect, we are yet influenced by, and are helping to bear the burdens of others. We cannot turn away. We are forced to stand and meet the issue face to face.

From a realistic point of view, there are many ways of looking at our present economic state. We

see our powerful and prosperous country with un-
diminished wealth and an oversupply of commodi-
ties, yet struggling in a slough of lack and unemployment that threatens to drain it of its very life blood.
Throughout the world we see governments being
overthrown and society undergoing disintegration.
Instead of getting into a panic over the seeming
hopelessness of the present conditions, we should revive our dormant faith that we live in a universe
governed by law, where nothing just "happens."
Back of every effect lies its cause. What kind of a
world would this be if such a holocaust as the late
World War could come and go without producing
any effect?

A still greater fundamental cause lies back of
war. We may trace it directly to the emotions in
the mind of the individual. Hatred, greed, jealousy, selfishness—all these have become manifest
conditions. The material world is a demonstration
of certain laws, causes, states of mind. Thought
energy always projects itself into form or expression.
If we would demonstrate profitably, our thought
should be positive and definite. It should agree with
the perfection of Divine Mind, which knows only
what is true. In every man's mind there are images
of achievement imprinted on his consciousness.
They are like seeds, holding within themselves infinite possibilities of development, growth, and fruition. Each produces its kind.

As individuals we have been planting wrong
ideals. We have been sowing to the flesh, and the

world of that flesh is reaping corruption. Too many
seeds of greedy exploitation have been cast into
the commercial plot. Too much impatience and
extravagance and excitement have been planted in
the social field. According to the universal law of
cause and effect these have "produced," and the harvest is chaos. The experience is already bringing
us back to a true realization of the meaning of
work. Lack of employment is making it desirable
not alone as a means of livelihood, but as a refuge
from apathetic indifference toward life.

It has been said that doubt comes from idleness;
that doing creates faith. I found a striking illustration of this in an article written by one of the lead-
ing educators of our day, L. P. Jacks, principal of
Manchester College, Oxford, and editor of the Hib-
bert Journal. Dr. Jacks says that work, once a sacred
thing, has become secularized. What was once an
expression of the spirit is now an exploitation of
materialism. In the days of paganism, every vo-
cation had a god or goddess to help and protect
the worker. Each deity was a master craftsman in
his particular line. He not only supervised the calling, but he worked at it. This certainly engendered
faith in the mind of the human worker. He could
believe in his god and the god's ability to help him
efficiently. It put divinity into his daily task and gave
him a motive for excellence of workmanship.

When Christianity first superseded the pagan religion, many of its gods and goddesses were transformed into patron saints. They were not so named,

of course, but their significance was the same. During the Middle Ages there were patron saints for every trade and calling, and many were the demands made upon them in times of trouble and difficulty.

It is far from Dr. Jacks's idea to suggest a return of paganism or to encourage a dependence on patron saints. What he does stress is his regret that men have lost their reverence for work. The worker once worshiped an ideal of excellence. Accomplishment created faith, and faith became an incentive to more and better work. "By works a man is justified, and not only by faith." It is a pity we have lost the vision of work as something divine manifested through human expression; that we have separated our works from our faith, our outer life from our inner spirit.

We need the revival of faith that shall bring about a reunion of the outer and the inner—a spiritualization of work, which is nothing more nor less than doing work in the best possible way. Emerson wrote, "Every man's work is his life preserver. I look on that man as happy who, when there is a question of success, looks into his work for a reply; not into the market, not into opinion, not into patronage. The man is happy who likes to see his work rightly done, for its own sake." What could be a better way than looking to the Master Craftsman who works always with the "son" for the uplifting and perfection of the ideal? Only the person who demonstrates his faith by accomplishment sheds inspiration abroad. His work declares his faith to the world.

It is easy enough to have vision; almost anyone may gain it. But vision will not abide with the man who does not believe in it enough to bend every effort toward working out its fulfillment. Persistent action must back it up, otherwise it is but a fleeting impression, not a vital conviction. I know of a man who built himself a cottage on the shore of a lake. Someone liked it and wanted to buy it. So the man sold it and built himself another. The same thing happened to the second one. He built another and another, and the demand for his cottages increased until quite a group had been built and sold. Someone suggested that a hotel was needed to complete the colony. One day the man was seen building a large chimney out in a cleared space. When asked why he was doing this, he answered that when he got the money he would build a hotel around it. Needless to say, the hotel was built. That is what I mean by working out a vision.

Instead of bemoaning the fact that there is no money or that we lack ability or that we have no opportunity, faith will impel us to step out into the seeming void. With skill and experience anyone can do the possible. Only the man of faith can perform the impossible. "Any man can see the farms that are fenced and tilled, the houses that are built. Only the man of faith sees possible farms and houses. His eye makes estates as fast as the sun breeds clouds."

Few of us have faith enough in our own capacities even to try what appears difficult. We wait for

someone else to blaze the trail for us. We try to do
only what has been done. We look only toward the
obvious. Every man has plenty of natural ability;
his mind would lead him out of worse troubles than
he is facing today if he would clear it of doubts and
fears. Every man can do this by cultivating the faith
that is perfected in "works."

Each man's business today is to contribute his
share toward regaining the lost morale of the world.
It is each man's duty as a citizen to "stir up the gift
of God" that is within him, to revive his faith in his
own capabilities, and to insure belief on the part of
those about him by demonstrating the confidence
that is his. For there are many now, as in the time of
Jesus, who are ready to believe "for their works'
sake" only. Each family or group or community or
country is composed of individuals whose attitude
as such produces the mass condition. This viewpoint places a responsibility upon every one of us.
Not one may stand aside in pathetic indifference.
Every man's faith must be made manifest in his
works. "To each one is given the manifestation of
the Spirit to profit withal." Nothing can take this
inner power away from him. Nobody can regulate
it but himself.

Even as physical bodies require exercise, so faith,
as mental muscle, must be developed through use.
This modern age demands of you and of me the
cultivation and application of that dynamic power
which must register in accomplishment. By our works
we shall be justified, and not by our faith only.

Every man must have faith, both in himself and in others. Each one must put his own house in order. Each must believe in his power and ability to do the works of Him that sent him into the world. Each must feel the responsibility of being a single cell in combination with all the other cells that compose the body of his community. Each must realize that no life ruled by the dynamic faith of spiritual insight can fail to get results. Each must know that in yielding himself unreservedly to the Spirit of good, he will be filled with its wholeness, which is perfection. We must expand our vision of world prosperity past all negative depression. We must cultivate the vision of faith that is made perfect in works.

We can do this by believing in ourselves and in our ability to overcome negative depression with positive, dynamic power; by seeking this power within instead of outside ourselves; by using it to crowd out inertia and discouragement from our thought, and by keeping sustained consciousness of the presence and power of God, and His ability and willingness to become flesh and dwell among us.

The Healing Principle

I T IS NOT EXAGGERATION to say that health is the most valuable thing we can have, and that we should use every effort to understand and demonstrate it. Physical health should be the most normal thing in the world, and yet it is estimated that the constant national average of those who are ill is two million daily. As we are living in an age of practical ideas, it is no wonder that the Christian religion has been challenged regarding the subject of healing. The modern slogan is usefulness, and men have very little patience with the dreams of idealists that cannot stand the test of workability. If an idea is not practical there is small needs for it in this era of civilization. For this reason people are beginning to feel that they have a right to demand of the gospel of salvation something that they can apply in their everyday lives; something that will help them solve their problems and adjust their difficulties.

One of the most perplexing of its problems, if not the most so, is that of ill health, and the Christian world is rallying as never before to the subject of healing. The founder of Christianity has always been called the Great Physician, but the true significance of this title has been lost in a maze of dogma and ecclesiasticism. Although twenty-four of the thirty-three miracles related as performed by the Nazarene were instances of the restoration of the sick to health, and although His instructions to His disciples were to preach and heal, with the passing of time the healing became separated from the preaching. In fact they grew so far apart that the very mention of healing in connection with religion was a declaration of fanaticism. Healing, in so far as its relation to Christianity was concerned, became a lost art.

As teachers of the Christ gospel got away from the pure and unmixed conceptions of the early church and began to emphasize doctrine as the basis of religious belief, the standard of the first Christians was gradually lost. Thus the healing of disease became ineffectual because of a loss of vision and of faith in the healing power.

With the advance of science, especially in medicine and surgery, it became quite natural for those who knew nothing of Christian ideals to depend on material means for the relief of physical ills. Humanity lost the meaning of the injunction of the Master to heal the sick as well as proclaim the gospel. The simple Truth principles that Jesus demonstrated in the "works" that He did, disappeared in a labyrinth of creed and dogma.

The Master emphasized the true authority of His teaching by definite physical effects. He was not satisfied to minister to the spirit and ignore the flesh. Those ministrations of His were joint healings of both mind and body. Few people realize that health includes more than just the flesh body. In fact it is news to most people that the body is but a result of mental and spiritual activity, and that that person is healthiest who best maintains a true balance among soul, mind, and body. Not many think of health as an expression of divine intelligence, a radiation of infinite energy, a liberation of God's activity. To Jesus, soul and body were inseparable and indistinguishable, but He refused to quibble with the learned theologians over an unimportant doctrine point. "Why reason ye in your hearts?" He asked of them. "Which is easier, to say, Thy sins are forgiven thee: or to say, Arise and walk?" He did not understand why they should stray so far from the point as to demand His authority to forgive sin and thus label His speech blasphemy.

The Nazarene, however, practiced His own preaching. Agreeing with His adversary quickly, He immediately expressed His Truth in a manner more to their liking. His "Arise, and take up thy couch, and go unto thy house" was the material demonstration of the real healing that had already been accomplished in the forgiveness of sin. If their primitive minds more readily understood a physical result than a spiritual cause, Jesus was willing to let them have it their way. He agreed with their ignorant demands that religious doctrine be omitted, and because they could not comprehend a spiritual remedy. He let them believe in a material "work."

To those minds of our own age whose doctrinal discussions act as barriers to the simple truth of Christianity, doubtless the phrase "forgiveness of sin" sounds fully as blasphemous as it did in the time of Jesus. However, a great creedal exodus is occurring. A mighty horde, passing through the sea of doubt and interrogation, is entering the land of Truth. Here its members are learning to understand the real meaning of that statement which to Jesus meant simply a removal of erroneous conceptions, a change of thought, a healing of the mind; the natural and logical result of this being a restoration of the body.

Jesus did not make the laws of healing. He discovered and proved them, giving to us His formula for applying them. We are rediscovering that science, and we are working in the firm belief that by following the methods prescribed by the Great Physician, we shall eventually do the work that He did; this work, and far "greater *works*" than this, according to His prediction.

The method of Jesus was based on Truth, which is pure science. Science is the discovery of the operation of law; it invades great strongholds of ignorance; it expands the general knowledge of humanity and cannot conflict with religion in its true sense. Jesus was a great scientist living, as He did, in close contact with the source of all knowledge, and His wisdom in using that knowledge made Him also a great philosopher. According to Jung, He is, "religion aside, the most perfect example of harmonized psychic activity the world has ever known." Perfection was His formula: perfection, through unity with the Father. How distinctly He emphasized this dependence on a power greater than the little human self! that self which, alone, accomplishes nothing, but which, co-operating with what He termed the Father, makes all things possible.

The idea of this Father or God as a deity with human emotions and impulses has been relegated to obscurity, along with ancient, outgrown superstitions and fanaticism. God is Spirit—Mind—Being. Descartes, the French philosopher, defined his conception of being in the words: "I think, therefore I am." In the old Testament record of Moses we find a statement quite similar to this. Moses, whose meekness is proverbial, was worried about his ability to assume the divine commission given him and asked what name he might give as authority. We read that God then said to him: "I AM THAT I AM: and he said, Thus shalt thou say unto the children of Israel, I AM hath sent me unto you." Moses was further instructed to say that I AM should be God's name forever, His "memorial unto all generations."

"Art thou greater than our father Abraham?" the Pharisees once demanded of Jesus. It was the Christ who replied, "Before Abraham was born, I am." This Christ who was with the Father before the world was, is in man proclaiming Himself as "I think, therefore I am." The words "I am" signify continuous Being; the immortal Spirit in man; the inheritance which he bears with him into this sphere of flesh and earth; his portion received when he was created in the image and after the likeness of God. This "I AM" or "being" is life, the One life that Jesus called the Father, the source of all existence.

Too long the world has believed in a God sepa-

rated and apart from man. It must come to know
that the universe is the sum total of divine existence;
itemized and individualized, it is true, but existent
only as a manifestation or expression of one Being,
the primal Life, the Father—God. It was Jesus the
scientist as well as Jesus the metaphysician whose
declaration "I in them, and thou in me" resounds
through the ages as a powerful principle; a principle
that He used continuously throughout His ministry.

The Great Physician performed His miracles of
healing by bringing humanity into a consciousness
of direct contact with this one and only life stream,
and by linking each lesser mind with its divine
source, connecting it with its central Spirit. He did
not begin with the materiality of the flesh. His diag-
nosis penetrated far beyond paralyzed limbs and
sightless eyes. These, to Him, were but changeable,
unsubstantial appearances. He worked with spiritual principle in His world of reality, the mind.

Many of our great scholars today are following
Him into that world. It is becoming more and more
conceivable that an external appearance exists only
in mind, and that man's perception of an outer manifestation is but an inference dependent on his inner
sensations. The late Camille Flammarion, dean of
astronomers of the last half century, in one of his
last books said that everything we believe is based
on illusion; that the earth we inhabit, which we regard as firm, fixed, and stable, is like a racing auto-
mobile, tearing wildly into space on an everascend-
ing spiral; that the ground beneath us is not fixed

and immovable, but is the surface of a planet rushing madly on its headlong course; that the earth itself is a plaything of fourteen different movements, and that it has never twice crossed the same path in space. He calls attention to the fact that our senses testify to a flat earth, not a round one; to a moon that is merely a silver disc in the sky; to light and sound vibrations sensed only by optic and auditory nerves. What we claim to know is merely what our senses tell us and these often play us false.

Ouspensky, the Russian mathematician, in his "Tertium Organum" points out that man is imprisoned in sense limitations and can have no true concepts based on material facts. Jesus was continually warning His followers and friends against belief in the false testimony of their senses. That Spirit of Truth which the world could not receive, that invisible friend and guide was the Mind of the Father expressing itself in the words of the Son whose perfect understanding made Him one with it.

The sense world is still crying, with Philip, "Show us the Father," and is loath to recognize anything as mysterious and unreal as a Father or Mind abiding within. That Mind, working through the Nazarene as absolute assurance, transcended all laws of a material universe. Its contact with the minds of men brought forth in them an innate God quality called faith. Its vision of spiritual perfection was so clear that it mirrored its images of health, peace, and plenty on that background of faith. Erasing the sins of fear, habit, worry, and misunderstanding, the vision was made manifest as health, happiness, plenty, even life itself.

Nothing that is perishable can be real. The physical body is not man's real self, for he is continually casting it off and as constantly renewing it. Of course, one may say that the body is real because it may be felt and weighed; it is substantial, active, hungry, thirsty. But it could be none of these without mind or Spirit. The real being, the I AM, is not physical. Life is a matter of consciousness, and the body is the instrument through which the mind functions on this earthly plane. The body is motivated and energized by the mind, which is the complete and perfect master to which it owes its very existence.

Many years ago Shakespeare wrote that "there is nothing either good or bad, but thinking makes it so." Thinking is the first manifestation of the living principle in man. It is that which flows forth into the body as expression. Employed constantly in one direction it becomes a "fixation" or habit. Disease is the result of habitual morbid or wrong thinking. This morbidity, which Jesus termed "sin," is not necessarily a continuous thought of sickness.

At a recent meeting of the world's most eminent surgeons, Dr. George W. Crile said that the control of the emotions is a general preventive measure that the individual must use against the destruction of his physical organism. He explained that a man cannot hate or fear or worry intellectually alone, because worry affects his whole body. Man himself lays the foundation for disease and ill health by failing to curb such agencies of devastation. It is agreed by most physicians that fear, especially, produces definite chemical results in the body, which can be clearly traced from the simple emotion to a result that may be characterized as, diabetes, for instance.

When we realize that the mind governs sickness and disease, we are on the way not only to rid ourselves of them, but forever to prevent their recurrence. We learn how to resist their attacks; how to treat them in their incipiency. Thus we can ignore their appearance and make them powerless to affect us.

The foregoing would be merely mental philosophy if we should fail to wield it to the religious motive. It is the purest form of Christianity, mastered by Jesus and practiced by His disciples and followers. We anchor our belief to it, for it justifies itself with all Truth. The Nazarene announced Himself as "the way, and the truth, and the life," and He proved Himself in all these capacities by the works that He did. He demonstrated Truth by teaching and by healing. Healing was an essential part of His system and as such He left it to His followers.

Most of us have been taught that Jesus' works were a proof that He was the Son of God, the second person in the Trinity, a sort of third fraction of God whose greatness divides itself into three persons. But we find Jesus telling Philip that those who believed in Him, those who had listened and learned through Him the method He employed should, because of their belief, accomplish even greater results.

Jesus the Christ revealed the possibilities of the finite mind when drawing on the Infinite. The power to perform the works that Jesus did has been neglected for centuries, but it has never been actually lost. It remains a law waiting to be employed. What one man has done another may do. Belief in the Christ in man has lost none of its vitality. It is as powerful today as it was in the time of Jesus, Peter, and Paul.

In the account given us of the healings of the Great Physician, we find that in some cases He supplied simple prescriptions—something the patient himself must do. It seems quite plausible that Jesus, by the art of suggestion, was but strengthening the faith of those who had always believed in the use of material remedies. For the dominant note in the healing work of the Nazarene was faith: "Thy faith hath made thee whole." "According to your faith be it done unto you." "Great is thy faith." "Thy faith hath saved thee." "As thou hast believed, *so* be it done unto thee." Each of these statements performed a miracle of healing. Certainly, faith is a quality of the mind or the spirit, the effective power standing behind all material remedies.

Heads of the medical profession today are emphasizing, as never before, the favorable influence of a happy, optimistic manner. The successful nurse or doctor must suggest buoyant, hearty well-being. "I bound up his wounds, but God healed him" is the inscription over the entrance to a great hospital.

This admission is coming to be general among
physicians today. The normal condition of the body
is one of soundness and wholeness, and we know
that nature always tends to assist and to upbuild.
Behind what we term nature there is, then, a something that is always ready to rescue and to heal.
The old idea that a pill or a poultice in some way
re-enforces this healing process or power is becoming threadbare. Intelligence is beginning to detect
flaws in the general practice of using material means
to make the action of the power easier. Mind is the
interpreting medium between life and its expression
in form. As mind ascends the scale of evolution it
repudiates those material aids, those queer little remedies that have but served as props to faith.

For it all goes back to the Master's principle: It
is your faith that heals you. Your healing comes
with the spiritualization of your mind, with the adjustment of your belief to the pure reason of God-
knowing. The Christ faith, dwelling in man, blots
out the errors or sins of his past; his recognition of
the Truth of his being, through unity with his Father, is bodied forth as perfection and according to
his faith he becomes whole.

Unfortunately man has wandered away from this
consciousness of his relationship with God, the principle of life and health. Like the prodigal son, he
must return. His awakening to the spiritual law
brings him into harmony with his Father and opens
new realms of thought to his mind. Through perfect ideas he develops latent faculties and, with the

spiritualization of his mind, he sees clearly and truly. Recognizing himself as the beloved of his Father, he casts away the husks of materiality, and feasts on the health-giving fruit of the tree of life, which is for the healing of the nations.

Our Real Body

THE BODY OF MAN is indeed fearfully and wonderfully made. In its physiological elements, its structural arrangement, and its mechanical processes, and in its adaptability to conditions, to influences and environment, it surpasses any machine in existence. Considered psychologically, it becomes not the solid mass of inert flesh it was formerly thought to be, nor yet the perfectly constructed mechanical device for functional activity; but a vibrant, intelligent cellular aggregation, capable of regeneration and renewal by means of its own elemental action. When we add to the physical and psychical, the spiritual conception of the body, thus seeking to unify all three, we have man as a divine microcosm, a little universe. Just as one drop of the ocean in miniature represents the whole, so man mirrors forth his divine parent macrocosm, God, the great universe.

Many years ago Plato wrote of a winged race of men upon the earth. This wingedness was symbolic, of course, of an ability to be free from the limitations of the physical body and to mount on the eagle's wings of poetic fancy high above the plane of sense. He conceived the soul as glued fast to the body and able to view existence through it only as through the bars of a prison. The flesh body he deemed a source of endless trouble as always requiring food and care, as liable to disease, as being instigated by fear and every sort of folly, and as being led through lust for gain to fighting, faction, and war. Not only this; as an enticer of the soul, he believed that it encouraged in it a belief in the reality of sense; every pleasure and every pain acting, as it were, as a nail clamping soul to body and fashioning it in the image of the material. He felt that it must end, perforce, in the soul's acquiring the nature and habits of matter.

It was the object of the Platonic philosophy to release the soul as much as possible from the deceitful perception of the senses, by withdrawing from them in so far as they might be dispensed with. Pleasures and desires, griefs, pains, and fears must be renounced as altogether evil. This ancient philosophy, though it rather encouraged the thought of release from the body as the great emancipator of the imprisoned spirit, contains invaluable wisdom.

Today we no longer count the loss of the body as something greatly to be desired. But we do need to learn to look inward for the real, and to close the senses to the outside world of the illusory. We must cultivate the ability to see with the inner eye the realities that endure and to recognize sensuous impressions as shadows, temporal, unreal, and evanescent.

In the Bible we find many seemingly inconsistent, contradictory statements concerning the body. It is called both vile and glorious; a temple of God, yet we read of Jesus casting devils out of it. We ponder over "celestial bodies, and bodies terrestrial" bodies corruptible and bodies incorruptible, and the subject seems to remain an enigma. We are continually asking, "How can these things be?"

Even though we read in our Scriptures that Jesus cared enough for His body to resurrect it, Christian martyrs have seen fit not only to neglect, but to deny and torture and mutilate it in the name of the Nazarene. How it has been mistreated and misunderstood!

Just as we have believed in the existence, side by side, of two powers, good and evil, so we have considered ourselves made up of two entities, soul and body. And it has been the mistaken belief that one of these is vile, while the other remains pure and perfect; that the soul is dragged downward and held captive by the material body in which it dwells.

It is quite evident that a more intelligent conception is needed. Not death but education shall set the soul free and dispel the illusions regarding it. The greatest factor in this educative process is an ability to see the body scientifically, as an objective manifestation of consciousness, as an individual expression of the idea man existent in Divine Mind.

When we speak of the soul being in the body, can it be that we mean it is inclosed there as a bird in a cage, or barred in as a prisoner in a cell, and that only the death of the body can free its captive spirit? Surely not. The soul is not something that is contained in the body and limited by it, as is commonly conceived. The body exists in the soul, although not in the sense of one object being circumscribed by another. It is what we mean when we say that God holds the universe in infinite consciousness.

According to the Platonic philosophy the individual man soul was formed out of the universal soul, and became a finite, personal limitation of its original source, and in the innermost man soul the body was formed. Regarded in this light the body exists as an indirect expression of the almighty consciousness and cannot be associated with weakness or limitation.

Owing to his ignorance of its true purpose, man has created a material, flesh body for himself. He has clipped the wings of his soul and imprisoned it behind the bars of sense. He can have no peace until he himself sets the captive free. When he does this he will know that man is not a flesh body resulting from a material conception, but a creation of Spirit, a manifestation of his own individual thought. "As he thinketh within himself, so is he." He cannot change his state of mind without automatically causing a corresponding change in his body.

When we grasp this fact we easily perceive its infinite, intrinsic possibilities, and we then understand man's body to be an orderly record of his self-discoveries, an outpicturing of his interpretation of the functions and powers that are originally his by divine right. These are all inherent in God-Mind.

It is a cosmic law that thoughts become things. It is the creative essence of all phenomena. Whether we believe it or not and whether our thoughts are adverse or harmonious, they objectify themselves and create the character of our surroundings. We cannot tell just how this recording of an idea is accomplished, any more than we can explain consciously how the heart beats or how the lungs breathe or how digestion and assimilation of food takes place.

The subconscious mind governs the body; for every phase of its development, whether physical, mental, or spiritual, has passed into the subconscious through the consciousness or awareness of the individual. An impression received and recorded enters the subconsciousness as a belief, and from that moment, whether it is true or false, it proceeds to exercise dominion. We see, then, how necessary it is to know the truth and to train the consciousness to allow no unchallenged thought to enter its realm.

The body of man is an effect, a manifestation of all that he has believed about it, an outcome of his consciousness, an externalization of the idea that his soul has formed of itself. It is thus a continuous creation of the mind, just as the soul is a perpetual creation of God. It would be foolish to deny the existence of the body, but we know that it has no independent existence. It continually derives its being from the mind. As a body it has neither life nor power. Without the consciousness that it expresses, it could do nothing. But, on the other hand, neither could the consciousness become expression without an organism. Mind and body must work together in fulfilling the divine purpose—the manifestation of infinite goodness.

So much for the original idea or divine plan. The human race has worked it out very differently. It has bound and limited its consciousness with error. It has believed in a material, corruptible, destructible flesh body; something that suffers pain and injury and dies. It has bequeathed this inheritance to every man. In attempting to free himself from what he feels to be a false conception, man has gone to the opposite extreme and denied his body, constantly thinking of himself as Spirit only; and this belief in separateness manifests itself as such unless it is given the protection of Truth principles.

The body is an individual record of thought, and identifies each person's interpretation of what he has "learned" through his physical senses. If he has believed in their report of the subconscious impressions of race thought, his body will publish the fact. The Truth found in Christianity destroys this belief concerning the body and discerns the real or "Lord's body" that is man's perfect identity in God.

In the infinite plan there was never such a creation as a body of flesh; there was no such manifestation as that which so tormented Paul with its contrary way of always doing as he "would not" and not doing as he "would." Man is continually perfect in Divine Mind. But our sense consciousness continues to read the thoughts of those about us as expressed in their bodies and, by the same sign, to recognize the change of thought as it manifests itself in altered bodies and different conditions. Concealment is impossible. There is nothing hidden away in a man's thought that is not revealed in his body and his life. He furnishes the mental model that his body images forth, and the bodily impression is a true representation of what he has chosen to think in his heart.

Paul's only solution to the problem that made him so wretched was in a transformation, a putting on of incorruption by the corruptible, of immortality by the mortal. The world's way of interpreting this transformation has been that it is completed only through the gateway of death. But the idea of waiting for death to free us from the vile flesh that we have called the body is the height of folly. The time to improve that body which we have is now.

All nature renews itself periodically. Man may use his relationship with nature thus to rejuvenate himself. As God creates the universe by divine ideas, so man may re-create his body by his governing thought. Every new and higher conception he forms will tend to an outward, bodily expression. This transformation must be wrought by the individual himself, and comes rather through the annihilation of ignorance and error than as the result of physical death. It may be accounted a mental resurrection, and it is man's privilege to rise from the grave of false thinking.

A delusion is a mistaken conviction, a persistent belief in something that is nonexistent. When the world of sense tells us that there is life, power or substance inherent in anything outside the infinite consciousness, it misleads our judgment. All sense delusion is based on a human belief that any life or intelligence can exist independently that is, apart from the mind of God. Sense delusion is a failure to discern spiritual reality, and it puts its trust in a lie. It believes that we see and hear with the eyes and ears of sense instead of those of the soul.

Through constructive thought we achieve mastery over sense delusion. To construct is to build; therefore constructive thought is a positive, conclusive, affirmative method of using the mind. It is God thought and, like it, creative. It releases the potentialities of the soul; it sets in motion innate and hitherto unrecognized faculties; it quickens bodily functions and harmonizes discordant physical effects. No one can think positively of himself as spiritually alive, well, happy, and abundantly supplied without building in his consciousness a vitalizing effect. Constructive thought is a sure way to achievement. It keeps us in sustained contact with infinite intelligence, and it teaches us to think in terms of reality.

Reality deals with the truly existing things, which are ideas. The reality of man is the sum total of God's ideas about him. He embodies those perfect ideas, although often but faintly, through his human limitation. His physical senses are always reporting the subconscious delusions of the race, and he sees in himself and others not the real or Christ man, but what each one is thinking about himself. Jesus refused to perceive anything but reality. He took away "the sins of the world" by not seeing its mistakes or criticizing its faults.

Jesus revealed the divine pattern of the body as a gift from the Father, a perfect, glorified creation, eternal in Mind. To Him the physical body was

never the real one, because He saw beyond it to the
permanent, spiritual idea existent in the infinite consciousness. If He had not so recognized it He could
never have demonstrated His power over it by overcoming death. In the Resurrection, He fulfilled the
divine likeness of man as conceived by the Father.

The record of Jesus' resurrection states clearly
that He assumed His natural body at will; the natural
body being that which was recognized by His friends.
For them He must still bear the image of the earthly,
because they could not yet discern His image of the
heavenly. "We know that, if he shall be manifested,
we shall be like him; for we shall see him even as
he is." Christianity reveals to us the resurrected or
spiritual body that, when it appears, opens our
inner eyes to a recognition of the "Lord's body"
and the inevitability of its purpose in the evolution
of the race. Christianity shows us that life is un-
foldment and must necessarily culminate in victory
over its last enemy, death. It indicates to us that
spiritual man is not without a body, but that his
body is not circumscribed by limitations super-
imposed by self-consciousness. It teaches us that the
kingdom of heaven is not entered through the gateway of death but over the top of the wall of limited
mortal beliefs, and that the spiritual realm is not a
different place, but a different condition.

We have said that thought is creative and that
all ideas clearly formed in mind tend to be material-
ized in the body; therefore the physical condition is
the material form of the dominant idea in the mind.

The development is not often instantaneous, rather it is progressive. It is not something finished but in the process of being accomplished or, as the Platonists would say, "in a state of becoming."

The mind works from any model we furnish it. If we hold steadfastly before it the divine idea and believe in its realization, it will re-create the body in accordance with its mental pattern. The body is healed only as the thought is healed. It is a true record of ideas and takes its own vengeance upon a miscreator. It must be spiritualized by the perception and recognition of its eternal perfection in Divine Mind. There is but one Mind, and the health of man's body, being in that Mind, can never be impaired or lost. When the concept of this spiritual body is revealed to man, healing becomes the most normal thing in the world. It is impossible for the body to manifest pain or disease if the thought which miscreated it is destroyed.

Let us seek to glorify God in our body by releasing from our mind the wrong beliefs we have held about it. Let us know that when we have dissolved this flimsy, material structure that we reared from a distorted, unsymmetrical model, we shall have "a building from God, a house not made with hands, eternal, in the heavens."

The All-Providing Power

THERE IS AN all-providing power that is limitless, unfailing, and inexhaustible. It picks
no favorites; for no man has been given
more than another. Each may have as much as he
demands, but his claim must be made in accordance
with recognized principle. He must look to an established law, that of action and reaction. Any
principle demonstrates itself when it is scientifically
and steadfastly applied. Once it has been put in
operation it works.

Everyone is looking for some providing power.
Few believe and trust in an all-providing source of
supply, a fountainhead of divine substance where
every need may be supplied and every desire fulfilled.
There are those who say they cannot believe in any
such intangibility, and there are others who feel that
material opulence should not be thus deified. They
are loath to associate substantial abundance with
anything approaching the spiritual side of life. It is
high time to get down to bedrock in dealing with this
subject, and to learn the fundamental principles by
which the problem may be worked out.

A mathematical problem contains its own solution, just as a block of marble holds a statue or a
violin promises divine harmony. The end has always
existed in the means *in potentia*. Pent-up volts in
the battery of Truth—unspent, unused forces—they
are there, subject to man's awareness, through his

mental connection with them. Until he himself makes the contact, they are of no value to him.

Man's point of contact with Truth is thought. Just as a defective connection renders the most potent electric current useless by preventing the completion of the circuit, so an untrue thought may short-circuit the stream of power that it seeks to employ. We must think according to Principle. We must know Truth, steadfastly and perseveringly, until we become mentally conscious of the divine Spirit that is the all-providing power that supplies every need.

When business conditions have so receded as to seem hopeless; when the negative expressions of lack and loss and failure have prevailed, and since their action has been so far backward, reaction is bound to swing the pendulum in the opposite direction with equal force. For every negative state, its positive reaction. Plenty in the same degree that lack appeared; gain in place of loss; success and prosperity equal in force and quantity to the discouragement and failure of their antecedent action.

Long before this reactive principle was a verified law of physical science, Paul wrote of established rules of action. Educated in Greek philosophy; scholarly even to the point of being accused of madness on account of his "much learning," Paul recognized law as a prime factor in man's existence. "Charge them that are rich in this world, that they be not high-minded, nor trust in uncertain riches," he admonished. "God shall supply every need of yours according to his riches."

This divine Spirit which meets all human needs, this Principle with which there "can be no variation, neither shadow that is cast by turning"; is it something for which we must sit down and wait? Does it imply that any effort toward self-reliance is useless? Have we so misinterpreted its meaning that we are patiently trying to endure lack and want until God notices our troubles and sees fit to bestow His largess upon us? If so, we may easily wait on and on until faith grows dim and we perhaps conclude that it is all a myth.

To be given the statement that God is substance and the source of all supply, seems worse than useless. We have also been told that He is Spirit, and He is not influenced by supplicatory appeals, and that He knows nothing about man's sorrowful problems. Is it any wonder that we are groping about in a chaotic bog of ignorance and despair, of discouragement and unbelief? Blind faith is not going to get us out, nor yet our agonized cries and earnest supplications. Understanding is the principle thing. Understanding is the well-spring of life that shall bring hope to a weary world.

The divine Spirit that will supply all our needs we have named God. And we have translated God as signifying true or spiritual consciousness. We mean by this that God—Spirit—is aware of creation in its absolute perfection. God consciousness is, therefore, true reality or unchangeable principle. The consciousness of man is his mental awareness of himself and the universe. Through this consciousness he cognizes Truth, which is knowledge of actuality. Knowing presupposes thinking, and true knowing implies true thinking or thinking in accordance with Principle.

The teaching of the Master was that knowledge of the Truth should make us free—free from all the false beliefs of the race that the sense man has reported as real. Man's responsibility is to know Truth, to think in spiritual principle. It is in this manner that God creates His universe, unhampered and unlimited by material restrictions. It is also in this manner that man achieves contact with the powerful mental battery of Truth.

An electric current may contain many volts of power, yet it will not run a motor or light a lamp unless certain specific connections are made. The mental battery of Truth is charged with limitless power—the inexhaustible supply of the universe. But man must not sit inertly waiting for the current to strike him in a thunderbolt of luck. Unless he is in connection with this stream of spiritual consciousness he can derive no benefit from it. But when the connection is made, he has at his disposal the unlimited force of the current of Truth. It is at his service. He may claim and employ as little or as much as he is willing to work for. Because some have claimed more than others is no reason for thinking them more highly favored.

The fact that lack and want persist in appearing in our lives is positive proof that we have not been thinking right. Poverty is the exact working out of mental error, the creation of negative, untrue thought. So we see how the attitude of serene waiting for God to notice and supply us is not only futile but actually destructive as well. For during this time we add the error of thinking more poverty, of worrying over delayed manifestation and withheld supply. These wrong conditions seem very real to us, and they will continue to hamper us until we no longer believe in their reality. Truth, being the only reality, we know the results of error to be false projections, externalizations of perverted truth.

That everything not of the kingdom is a lie was the teaching of Jesus. Lies may appear very genuine, and often we have accepted them as true and right conditions because we have not sensed their false appearance. As we recognize their unreality we remove their power to become manifest in our affairs. Spiritual understanding, right thought, must reveal their identity and their failure to measure up to actuality.

Many will resent the statement that lack and want are evidences of wrong thinking; they will say it cannot be true. It is a very human trait to shirk responsibility and to shift blame. We do not relish having attention called to our faults. But whether we like it or not, Principle proves itself. Thought is causative, creative. Any habitual thought establishes itself in consciousness as a mind model. Once it is firmly fixed there, its externalization is certain. Sometimes we are born with wrong mental prototypes or mind models; with false ideas of poverty and inherited ill health. We can change these if we learn and apply and persevere in a knowledge of Truth.

The father of Andrew Carnegie was a Scottish weaver, in the day of the hand loom. The machine age was even then beginning to intimidate the weak and unprogressive. Steam was making its defiant entrance. When it crowded out the hand looms, Carnegie senior could not contend with it. "There is no work," he reiterated. "There is no use praying, there is nothing to be thankful for. Prayer will not abolish the steam factory. There is no work." "Then we will go where there is work," the mother of a future multimillionaire decided.

Andrew Carnegie, then a lad of eleven, was his mother's son. At that age he began to work where work was to be found—in America. He changed the Carnegie mind model from "There is no work" to a word that became a recognized synonym for the word Carnegie. That word was "Work," and it guided Andrew Carnegie throughout his life, in much the same manner as it interested and attracted another brilliant Scottish mind, that of Thomas Carlyle. Dissatisfaction with the mind model of poverty resulted in one of the world's greatest fortunes. Habitual knowing that lack was a wrong idea, that "No work" was a false mental creation, changed both the environment and the condition of Andrew Carnegie.

Every negative thought, however seemingly inconsequential, may become destructive if it is received into consciousness. Human opinions and be-

liefs, such as worry, criticism, condemnation, jealousy,
and failure all contain germs of growth and development. If they are nourished by encouragement they
will become externalized as negative conditions.
They will develop into imperfect manifestations of
annoyance. When we say, "This is too good to last,
it cannot go on indefinitely, there is bound to be a
slump," such emphatic predictions must have a natural consequence. Negative vibrations of disaster
will influence the mind until a strong consciousness
of fear develops. Fear will grow into panic and
panic will embody itself in failure.

We have to find the true source of prosperity.
We have to know that this can be done only through
active effort and according to fixed principle. Who
believes that unlimited supply is the gift of God?
Who has the firm conviction that this gift has been
bestowed upon him? Not one in a thousand. *Every
man is supplied according to the riches he has in
mind.* The demonstration of this supply depends
on how clearly he sees it and how persistently he
thinks it. To some it comes as a swift revelation;
others advance gradually toward the truth.

If you cannot picture your supply as illimitable,
if you cannot believe your heritage to be "all that the
Father hath," begin with smaller mind models of
substance. Increase them gradually. Know with Coué
that "day by day, in every way" they are growing
greater and greater. As this knowledge becomes a
part of your consciousness it will act as a magnet
to draw to your life the rich substance of God.

"All things whatsoever ye pray and ask for, believe that ye receive them, and ye shall have them." The principle is that good must be claimed, incorporated in thought, made a part of our very being. It must become such a firm conviction that we shall never say or think, "I am poor; I can't afford this." Not that one should squander one's substance, whether its manifestation be large or small.

The question of spending is a puzzle to many. Is it wise to pay out lavishly when there is seeming lack? Should one give all that one appears to have? While it is wrong to think you cannot afford to do or to have what you desire, if you indulge in reckless extravagance your mind will perhaps tell you that now you have nothing, and your last state will be worse than your first. If this idea becomes a mental model it will work itself out in your affairs.

There are those with great riches who impoverish themselves by giving out, because they cannot let go of their possessions; because they are constantly picturing to themselves how much they have given or spent, and how much less they now possess. And there are those who seem to have very little, as compared with vast wealth, who enrich themselves by even the smallest expenditure, because they know that "the one base thing in the universe" is "to receive favors and render none." They have learned with Emerson that "too much good staying in their hand . . . will fast corrupt."

Truth always has been. Truth is now. Truth always will be. It is the divine Spirit, the all-providing

power that supplies every human need. In it is substance—the very breath of all mankind. Truth is
in and all about us. It remains in a static condition
until we apply the dynamic force of mind, which is
the connecting wire over which the providing power
moves. The power is limitless, inexhaustible, dependable. As long as we furnish a proper conduct-
ing medium, the full capacity of its operating energy
is ours. It is our responsibility to keep the channel
open and to cleanse it of all error thoughts so that
the mighty current of spiritual consciousness may
flow through us and manifest itself in our lives as
the perfect gift of God.

Through spiritual education we learn to free our
individual powers. We deal with ideas only, not
with external objects. Christianity furnishes spiritual
principles whereby we may discriminate between
what is true and what is false. "Ask, and it shall be
given you; seek, and ye shall find; knock, and it shall
be opened unto you: for every one that asketh re-
ceiveth; and he that seeketh findeth; and to him
that knocketh it shall be opened." After you have
asked, sought, and knocked, keep on believing that
you have received. You have not influenced the all-
providing power by asking, seeking, and knocking.
What you have desired has always been yours, but
through the activity of your effort you have put yourself in condition to receive it. Your asking has assumed the willingness of God to give, and declared
your readiness to receive, your divine inheritance.

The Law of Compensation

SOONER OR LATER we come face to face with the law of compensation and its assurance that, inevitably, our own comes to us and only what is our own. Back through the evolutionary stages there has always been this law of compensation, holding "different gifts to different individuals, but with a mortgage of responsibility on every one." As we apply it to life and watch its certain manifestation, do we find a counterbalance for the effort of living? Are we satisfied with the benefits we are receiving? Are we getting fair returns from our investment? Do we feel that "our own" has come to us? Most of us are dissatisfied and believe that it has not. Many say that life is not worth the living. The great majority declare that injustice is rampant in the world and more especially in their own individual lives; that sickness, poverty, and unhappiness stalk undiscriminatingly through human existence.

Every person would like to believe in a magic power that could give him what he feels are his just deserts in life. Nearly every person places a high valuation upon these "deserts" and feels that if justice were dealt him, he should receive the very best that life has to offer. There is really nothing egotistical in such an assumption; for man as the divine son has a perfect right to regard "all things whatsoever the Father hath" as his heritage—to expect them as such. But few understand why this is true.

"The world owes me a living," you hear one say, often with a reckless determination to collect the debt in whatever way proves the easiest. "I don't deserve this" or "How unjustly Fate has dealt with me" are common expressions of defeat or failure. "Why should this person have everything, while I, who have a better right to it, have nothing?" This is an oft-repeated query.

The old and let us hope obsolescent religious teaching was that justice might be expected only in some other life. The rich and powerful, assumed to be wicked and overbearing, were bound to receive punishment after death; while their unfortunate victims, being poor and wretched but devoted to religion and the church, were sure to be bountifully rewarded in an after life. No such attitude is ever permissible from the viewpoint of Truth.

The word compensation rests upon a basis of immutable principle, suggesting counterbalance or equality of opposing forces, and it leads directly to an established rule of physics—that of action and reaction. This is a law that we come in contact with daily and it grows with our awareness. Nature emphasizes it as darkness and light, ebb and flow, heat and cold, male and female. Science presents it as the polarity we recognize in contrasts—attraction and repulsion, cause and effect, subjective and objective. Religion teaches it as spirit and matter, good and evil, God and Devil. We meet it continually as wisdom and ignorance, sickness and health, poverty and riches. Jesus included it as a supreme factor in

His doctrine. "Give, and it shall be given unto you." "Judge not, that ye be not judged." "With what measure ye mete, it shall be measured unto you." And Paul said, "Whatsoever a man soweth that shall he also reap."

The sooner we come to know and apply the just law of compensation the sooner we shall realize that we are but reaping what we have sown, if not on this plane, then on a former one. The difficulties we are encountering have not been sent by an angry God as punishment, or by a vindictive power seeking vengeance. Our suffering is of our own creation, and those who will not so consider it must remain in a state of chaos. Refusal to meet the issues in this life simply means a postponement, carrying them forward into the next, where they may prove even greater hampering barriers. The burden of time-worn obligations becomes heavier; old debts grow harder to pay; procrastination neither reduces nor cancels our liabilities. Sooner or later they must be met in their entirety.

It is not necessary to accept the theory of reincarnation to believe in the immortality of the soul and its progress throughout eternity. It is reasonable to interpret the Master's description of the Father's house of many mansions as significant of many degrees of consciousness through which the individual soul must pass. The school of life has many classes, the drama of being many scenes. The brief term of this earthly existence is but one grade, one short scene in a series. Who can judge the great whole by one of its parts? Other episodes have been experienced; many more will follow.

Some of us have failed in past examinations, bringing with us into our new grade held-over subjects to be made up, conditions to be adjusted—in the form of unrighted wrongs, unforgiven sins, unpaid debts of love and kindness. Nothing can remain hidden. No lesson may go unlearned. Every debt must be paid. When these obligations are revealed, when they present themselves for settlement in myriad forms, when perhaps early in the new plane of existence payment is demanded, we bitterly rebel at what seems utterly unjust to us. Physical ills, mental disturbances, financial difficulties, loss, failure, and criticism—against all these we cry out. Cruel injustice has been perpetrated. Why should these things come to us when we have never done any wrong to deserve them?

Whatever we possess today is our just desert; we have sown it and the harvest belongs to us. Very often it does not make us happy. We are dissatisfied with it, but it remains ours. This fact would prove hopelessly discouraging were it not for a great truth that teaches us how to be free from difficulty, released from bondage, absolved from debt.

God as infinite law is both the bountiful giver of all good and the dispenser of divine justice. Man as an individualized expression of that absolute good is a user of God power. All our lives we have been employing this creative capacity. How have we directed it? What have been our thought patterns? If we are continually rebelling against the fact that our own has been kept from us, that another has been given our rightful place, that money and position have been unjustly snatched from us, it is time to pause and take an inventory of our past.

The majority of people, if they are strictly honest with themselves, can find a balance of profit on hand. The law of compensation is at work everywhere, and those who feel they have the least in life for which to be thankful often wake up to the fact that they have the most, and that seeming deprivation has been counterbalanced by an equivalent blessing.

In striking the balance sheet of life it is expedient to take stock of what has been invested of Truth and error, of harmony and discord, of sickness and health, of poverty and riches, of unemployment and work. Every thought is living capital and brings forth dividends for its investor after the manner and kind of the investment made.

If you feel that your business of living is bankrupting you, know that there is a way of canceling all your debts. Learn your lesson. Pay your obligations. You need not wait for another lifetime or depend on a future incarnation. Draw now upon the currency that is yours. That portion which rightly belongs to you will come to you if you recognize infinite justice in the compensatory law. What you invest will return to you, what you sow you shall reap, what you give out will come back to you. It seldom returns directly from one particular investment; rarely will you reap just where you have sown; al-

most never will your requital come from the person
who is in your debt. But the divine law is in constant operation to bring you what and all that is your
own. Infinite justice cannot make mistakes.

If you are sick, poor, or unhappy and you feel
that bitter injustice is being done you, you must know
that every fear thought draws compound interest of
worry; every disease thought manifests itself as ill
health; every idea of lack and limitation pays a poverty dividend; criticism, condemnation, and jealousy
result in unhappy discord; rebellion and resistance
close the avenues of supply and keep your good far
from you by accentuating the power of adverse conditions.

On the other hand, courage is transformed into
confident faith. Love shines forth as joyous harmony.
Every positive idea of wholeness is a creative force
bringing health into operation. Every seed of
opulence produces its harvest of plenty. Today we
are reaping conditions produced by past thought
forms. Today we are sowing seed for future gar-
nering. What we put into life is our own and nothing can keep it from us. With unerring exactitude it
returns to us.

No substantial business is established overnight.
No harvest develops in a day. It takes more than
one lesson to become an expert. Just so the business
of living requires painstaking attention to every investment. Life's garden must be planted and watered and encouraged to grow. Lessons in the school
of the world must be learned, one by one—worked

out from a scientific basis and according to principle.

We hold in the subconscious mind the errors of the race thought, its fears and delusions, its doubts and misgivings. They will continue to be reproduced in our bodies and affairs until their power has been destroyed. Only Truth can nullify their destructive effects. As long as an evil is retained in the subconscious mind we cannot be rid of it; hence its beliefs in sin and sickness, poverty and lack, injustice and failure must be corrected. They can be eliminated only by our insight into Truth, which is correct thinking. It is impossible to think both correctly and incorrectly at the same time; therefore as the true idea appears in consciousness, it is recorded in the subconsciousness and crowds out old beliefs with their disastrous consequences. Since our bodies and affairs are automatic reproductions of the subconscious mind, and it is an automatic record of that which the conscious mind accepts as fact, we should train the consciousness to know its power. No thought should be allowed to pass unchallenged, no belief unsubstantiated.

With the advent of the talking picture a curious bugaboo arose. It stalked beside youthful inexperience and seasoned maturity alike, terrifying the timid actor, baffling the sagacious, and undermining the assurance of even the most confident egotist. The name of this uncanny specter is "fear-of-the-microphone," and it interposes its shape between many an artistic conception and its expression. This panic producer is an accurate recorder of sound.

Nothing escapes its exactness of reproduction on the sensitive film of that which comes within its range of "hearing." Whether pleasant or discordant, whether meant for recording or accidentally interpolated, the film holds a correct record.

There could be no better illustration of the recording power of the human consciousness, and we should be just as vigilant regarding that which passes through it to the subconscious mind as the director is when he gathers his vibratory material for the microphone. The delicate film of the subconsciousness receives the impress of what has entered the scope of consciousness. Like the terrifying microphone it "listens" to what is allowed within the range of its attention, and it cannot of itself discriminate between the pleasing and the discordant. Man stands in the role of director. He has the intelligence to select material that will make his life rich with harmony or mar it with discord.

Why then, with such a simple formula, do we lack anything that is good? We often say and honestly believe that we have had no part in the disaster that overtakes us. We feel that we are victims of circumstance or that luck is against us. We accuse others of having defrauded us, and we bitterly denounce them, declaring justice to be a myth or a huge joke. But if we are truly seeking a way out, if we are really candid with ourselves, some of us must admit that we spend more time and energy in fear and worry, in anticipating pain, loss, and lack, in limiting ourselves and human conditions than we do in

expressing life, health, happiness, and prosperity.
When the law manifests its power, when our own
comes back to us, how we rebel and resist and labor
as we beat against it!

"Resist not" was the Christ law, stressing the idea
of never retaliating. We must stop fighting conditions, cease wasting strength in futile rebellion. Re-
sentful cries of injustice bring no response; they tense
and tighten and block all channels through which
help might come. Jesus was able to maintain the pure
God consciousness that the world cannot touch.
He was confident of the spirit of absolute justice
within. He was a perfect exemplification of the employment of God power.

"My Father worketh . . . and I work." "The
Son can do nothing of himself, but what he seeth the
Father doing." "As the Father hath life in himself,
even so gave he to the Son also to have life in himself: and he gave him authority to execute judgment." Could anything be clearer than the Master's explanation of God's working through man as
divine activity? and of man, as the expression of that
activity, with authority to judge how to employ it?

Spiritual laws are eternal verities and must work
out according to Truth. A principle inevitably demonstrates its own exactness as a rule of action. Justice is a divine law that tolerates no violation. Justice decrees for man health, happiness, and abundance. But justice does not bring forth figs from
thistles. If man disobeys the rules of health, harmony, or supply, the law of compensation becomes

manifest. Misuse of the power that makes him well, happy, and prosperous when correctly and intelligently employed, reacts according to principle in sickness, inharmony, and poverty.

We have been given authority to execute judgment in life, to choose our method of procedure. The God power is infinite, and through its expression all things may be ours. Every time we choose a thought of wholeness we make a health investment. Every idea of substance draws compound interest. Every vision of reality is a share of preferred stock in the kingdom of happiness.

What is life paying you today? Health or disease, happiness or misery, lack or abundance? Whatever it is, it is your own. It belongs to no one else. You have made the investments and you are drawing the interest. If you are dissatisfied with your dividends, begin now to withdraw your capital fund. Change your investment. Watch every thought. Guard your conscious mind against the intrusion of error and its subsequent entry into the subconsciousness. Be true to the dominion entrusted to you.

There is a law of health; learn and obey it. There is a formula for happiness; follow it. There is a principle of plenty; comply with it. Only your own can come to you, and be sure that all that is yours will become manifest. It is your responsibility; no other person may share it. Your own, only your own, and all of your own will come to you.

The Eternal Goodness

THERE ARE various ways of looking at life, and inevitably our viewpoint colors our outlook and determines our course. Many are seeing "in a mirror, darkly" all sorts of distorted conditions of error and evil for themselves and others. The universe to them is dark and dreadful, and life confuses and baffles them. But there are others and their number is daily growing whose wisdom, "face to face" with true reality, sees clearly. We may define the dim obscurity of that shadowy glass through which the majority are peering as ignorance of principle, causing spiritual shortsightedness.

If you have ever driven through thick fog, you know how it restricts the view and distorts familiar objects along the roadway; how it closes in and circumscribes the range of vision, concealing the beauties of vista and perspective. Even your headlights do not pierce it, indeed their light is often reflected back upon you and increases your difficulty. Until the fog lifts there is no clarity of vision.

It is just so with ignorance, and by ignorance I do not mean illiteracy. The most learned person may still be ignorant of many things. His knowledge of the objective world may be accurate, systematic, and to a certain degree complete. But without wisdom he propels his life through a fog of ignorance that accepts the limitations of evil and error and that cannot get beyond the petty personal point of view. Until the fog is dispelled the ignorant mind faces an incomplete universe.

Such ignorance harks back to the early days of civilization when primitive man regarded the universe as hostile; when he read enmity in all of nature's forces and sought to protect himself from its destructive intent. As his life was a continuous battle with the elements, he believed himself to be a target for the fury of storm and flood, an insignificant atom to be overwhelmed and destroyed by forces that he was powerless to combat and that were constantly seeking to annihilate him.

This fear of things that he did not understand was very likely the beginning of man's religious inclinations. Something within him felt the need of a power greater than his own to protect him from the antagonistic malevolence of nature and the clutch of painful disease. In his primitive ignorance he cried out to it for help, and he thought to secure its favor by bribery or to buy off its evil intention by sacrifices and the payment of tribute.

When the power that he invoked failed to respond to his placating efforts, his groping mind gradually established a reason, and thus the idea of punishment was born in his consciousness. He grew to believe in a power that dealt out disaster, disease, and death in return for certain acts that he learned to call wrong or evil. And so his personal god took shape as a ruler of the universe and its forces who rewarded merit and punished delinquency.

As man's intellect evolved and his knowledge became embodied in system, science arose as his interpreter of the natural universe. Science has transformed the world for him. Its brilliant illumination has dispelled the terror that his dark ignorance of nature's activities inspired in primitive man. It has proved beyond a doubt that the universe is not unfriendly and revengeful, seeking to entrap and injure human beings, demanding bribe and sacrifice from them, and imposing punishment upon them.

But it has done more than that. It has shone upon an anthropomorphic God and revealed the unreliability of a finite deity. The necessity has arisen for re-establishing omnipotence. The mind of today must have a "court of appeal" that is infinite both in power and integrity. Through research and hard experience man has acquired a new idea of the universe and its trustworthy, orderly method of operation. He has rejected his earlier conclusion by which he once judged nature to be incomplete and imperfect, subject to capricious uncertainty and the unpredictable occurrences of mere chance.

Ignorance still labels life a failure, regarding it as empty and purposeless, lacking in health, supply, and intelligence. It points to sickness, unhappiness, incompetence, and failure. But knowledge that is born of intelligence and directed and guarded by wisdom looks upon an orderly, harmonious world, a perfection of wholeness in which no division or duality exists, where there is no good *and* evil, no truth *and* error, where nothing is accidental, and where the old illusions and superstitions of ignorance have been corrected by scientific study. It reads divine order in the regularity of the tides, in the unchanging sequence of day and night, season and cycle, and in the mathematical precision of starry progress throughout the celestial sphere.

Terror of sudden catastrophe has been calmed by the scientist's assurance that an essential uniformity of cause and effect, forces and phenomena has prevailed in all ages of the world's physical history. He calls attention to the laws of motion and gravitation, of action and reaction, of vibration and growth, and the dependable and trustworthy way in which they perform their various functions.

We know that from the tiniest atom to the farthest reaches of the celestial sphere "the world was built in order, and the atoms march in tune" to the uniform rhythm of design. We have such faith in this substantial, methodical activity, that we never doubt the sun will rise in the east, that seasons will change according to schedule, and that lunar and solar eclipses will come and go according to exact computation made many years in advance. To every exerted force there is an equal response. In every seed is a potential harvest. Every word spoken into the ether vibrates throughout all space. As we harmonize with nature's forces we discover not a hostile resistance seeking to destroy, but a friendly power co-operating to transform life and work always in behalf of our best interests.

But man must learn to understand and agree with elemental forces, otherwise they may disturb and even destroy him. I was once very close to a vast, raging forest conflagration in the Canadian Rockies. As it swept in a sea of flame on its destructive course, reducing beauty to ashes, it was hard to realize that fire is one of our greatest blessings and that the discovery of its use marked an epoch in the evolutionary story of civilization.

Again, when I watched gigantic waves of the Caribbean rising mountain-high and for days breaking over the great ship I was on, making it appear by comparison a very frail shelter, I could scarcely associate such pounding fury with the life-giving water, so necessary to man's existence upon the earth. And there is the angry force of the air beating and lashing that which lies in its path to resist it, yet it is indispensable to mankind. How marvelously man has learned through understanding to employ all of nature's forces advantageously and to rely upon them for service that is friendly, so that he may regard the world as Robert Louis Stevenson saw it: "a very joyous and noble universe, where any brave man may make out a life that shall be happy for himself and beneficent to those about him."

But man himself stands as his own interpreter between the abstract spirit and the concrete material world. His translations are wise or ignorant as he chooses to make them. The wise man thinks according to principle and recognizes the allness of good. He seeks this allness within his own soul, knowing that, without mind, matter would have no existence. Immanuel Kant saw the material world as "an appearance, a sensuous image; a picture swimming before our present knowing faculty like a dream and having no reality in itself."

The ignorant mind looks at this appearance and believes in its reality. It sees imperfection and evil and continually grants power to sickness, unhappiness, and failure. The mind guided by reason sees a totality of good; but ignorance recognizes division and duality, recognizing both good and evil.

From the human standpoint these two great opposites have always been taken for granted. We get the idea of sin early in life as a part of the ritual of baptism. It robs us of our true birthright, which is not that of children "conceived and born in sin" but of sons of God and heirs to His kingdom of all good. We speak glibly of good and evil, feeling that one is to be desired, the other resisted; but how often do we pause to ask ourselves what they represent to us?

When we repeat, "All is good," is it a platitude or something we know rationally and are able to cling to and depend on in times of difficulty and danger? Is it merely an abstraction or is it a practical truth? We think of evil as something characterized by calamity, trouble, or sorrow that prevents our enjoyment of life. It obscures our vision, concealing the good that is ever present as completely as though it did not exist.

We think of sickness, sorrow, and poverty as evil. What is sickness but a lack of health, sorrow but a lack of joy, poverty but a lack of supply?

Evil, then, is always associated with lack, and lack is something that is *not*. Lack can only be filled by that which *is*. When we try to define what is, there is but one word for its expression: Truth.

Truth is that which is absolute, unlimited, complete, and perfect; not what seems to be or what we believe to be, in relation to something else. It is what is, absolutely, and it is all there is, for the reason that nothing can exist except what is. What is not is a nonentity, without existence. Truth is indivisible. We cannot compromise with it or divide it into parts. It is all or nothing, inseparable, unchangeable, absolute. However substantial a thing may appear to be, it is not real if it is subject to change. No one can believe in evil as an everlasting quantity or condition; it has no stability, is continually changing, and must finally disappear altogether.

If Truth is all there is, it must be all positive or all negative, all good or all evil. It is unthinkable to speak of Truth as all evil, for then evil would be a permanent state of being. If Truth is all there is and evil is not, good must be Truth. In recognizing the allness of Truth, then, we substantiate the statement that all is good.

As we have interpreted evil to indicate a sense of lack, we now define its opposite, goodness, as wholeness or completeness. It is that which lacks nothing because it is all. We can readily understand that the basic principle of good is that which we call "God," even though we use the word lightly, often thoughtlessly. We speak of a good drawing, good music, good weather, and good food. What we mean to convey is that whatever is good is completely what it is represented to be: pure, unadulterated, thoroughly whole, free from lack, and entirely satisfying. A good drawing is perfect in line and perspective; good music is free from discordant jangle; good weather is neither too wet nor too dry and neither too hot nor too cold; good food is that which satisfies.

People are clamoring for jobs not because they like to work, but for the money they receive. Money, however, fails to gratify them unless they are miserly hoarders, obsessed by a golden glitter. Money is a means of possessing the food and clothes, warmth and shelter, leisure and amusement that give satisfaction. The things that satisfy and comfort him are the things the job seeker really wants and they are to be found only in the principle of infinite good.

The old idea of goodness with its puritanical conceptions of right and wrong was associated with a kind of martyrdom. In order to be good one was required to sacrifice everything interesting or amusing; all pleasure was labeled wrong; right and good were associated with duty and dullness. But we have come to realize that goodness is a big word. It includes many attributes and is a synonym for all that implies completion and perfection. It is wisdom and knowledge, power and freedom, love, joy, peace, health, wealth, and rightness.

There can be no implication of dullness in a collective consciousness of what goodness really is.

A good life is full, whole, complete, lacking nothing that promotes joy and satisfaction. Every worthy want has already been supplied, but unless we abide by the conditions of its fulfillment we cannot hope to see its manifestation.

As long as man dwells upon his own self-righteousness, blaming other people or conditions, or God perhaps, for his troubles, this is going to hamper and enslave him. Self-righteousness believes in a human, self-made goodness and is the root of self-pity. Its egotism sees only the injustice and lack of appreciation in others. It believes and says, "All these things have I kept from my youth up [and I have done them rather well, yet I have never been rewarded for my excellence!]." This kind of righteousness has nothing to do with man's belief in his divine goodness.

"Why callest thou me good?" were the Master's words. *"There is* none good but one, *that is,* God." Goodness cannot be personalized, or individualized. Man is good only as he opens up his heart and mind to the eternal goodness and lets it become manifest through him by becoming one with the infinite principle of good. When he does this, evil is erased from his consciousness and ceases to hold any reality for him. One by one all troublesome conditions drop away, as he learns to turn within and see good only.

"To this end have I been born, and to this end am I come into the world, that I should bear witness unto the truth," namely to that which is—God, the eternal goodness. Man bears witness to this by translating abstract principle into concrete expression through his creative thinking, and thus he changes world events.

We have seen that Truth is, and that it is all there is. Goodness then, being Truth, is all-powerful. Think what this means! There is no power in any of the things we have feared; no real power to harm or trouble us. They have done so only because we have refused to exercise our intelligence. We have given power to the body, allowing its wants and imperfections to torment and torture us. But the body is a reproduction of what we have believed about it and has no power except that which it gets from the consciousness of which it is an expression.

Intelligence tells us that power is not centered in the effect but in the cause, and that we must begin by applying principle to the consciousness. Healing of the body is accomplished first in the mind, by erasing the belief that conditions can in any way affect the allness of good which is Truth. As the idea of pain or disease is removed from the mind, neither can be experienced even though they may present themselves to the senses. On the other hand, an idea firmly fixed in the mind must always gain concrete expression through the consciousness.

We have given power to personality, allowing the feelings and opinions of others to influence and rule us. Our idea of goodness is permanent satisfaction—that which is secure and unchangeable. But personality is changeable, unreliable, unsatisfactory, and having no permanence, it cannot measure up to the truth of eternal, universal goodness.

Good is the only power in the universe. It is the almighty, creative principle within each soul, capable of unlimited expression in the life of humanity. It is what man was designed to prove as Truth, to manifest as reality, and to experience as satisfaction or completion. The desire for satisfaction is the soul's longing for God or All-Good. "My people shall be satisfied with my goodness, saith Jehovah." "Their soul shall be as a watered garden; and they shall not sorrow any more."

Like a productive garden, man must yield his goodness for the benefit of others. He must give it out and relieve the lack that has fixed itself in the racial consciousness and expressed itself in evil conditions. "Whatsoever ye would that men should do unto you, even so do ye also unto them." If you would receive goodness, you must give it out. This does not mean dispensing charity or exercising personal generosity. Man gives out goodness by changing his belief in himself; by putting off the absurd old idea of sin and evil and putting on "the new man," with his belief in omnipresent, omnipotent, beneficence; by realizing his own power to create conditions and thus transform his entire world. He must grasp the real meaning of power and his ability to exercise it, knowing that he himself is responsible for his own unhappiness and failure, through his ignorance of principle.

Unity

A BRITISH prime minister addressing Parliament, once said: "Gentleman, we must study larger maps." The trouble with the world today is its failure to see life clearly because of the inability to see it as a whole. Our vision is limited by our proximity to this or that phase of life, which prevents a true interpretation of life's full meaning. Until we are able to enlarge that vision so that we may see, not merely what is obvious and superficial, but the vast magnificence of the totality of the whole, we shall miss the great things that a more extended vision would reveal to us. We must seek larger, more comprehensive, vistas. We must rise with spiritual wings above separateness and disagreement until, like the aviator, high above the earth, we can extend our perspective to include vast spaciousness. As we rise higher and see farther, the petty boundary lines that we have drawn vanish, and "larger maps" stretch before us.

The world that we are living in seems to have lost its way. In the midst of its man-made, chaotic conditions, with confusion all about, when everything appears to have gone awry and men are groping in a maze of disagreement and inharmony, the revelation of a great mind very often flashes encouragement. Such stimulation was given very recently, as the result of an attack made upon Professor Einstein's theory of relativity by one who declared it to be noth-

ing less than a cloak for atheism. Einstein was asked
if he believed in God. His reply was illuminating.
"I believe in Spinoza's God," he said; "a God who
reveals Himself in the orderly harmony of His universe; not a God who concerns Himself with the little actions and disagreements of individual human
beings."

We can do no better than to base our science of
life on the formula of that seventeenth-century sage,
the founder of modern philosophy, called by Novalis
the "God-intoxicated man," and chosen as the ideal
religious guide of an Einstein intellect. For Spinoza,
looking at the manifestations of nature, saw one
supreme cause back of them all. He began where
you and I must eventually begin, with God. His interpretation of deity led him to a scientific conclusion that pointed to a unity of purpose, an orderly
harmony, existent in a unified whole.

In this universe, which is alive from center to
circumference, omnipresent Spirit is the inspiration
of all manifestation, both animate and inanimate.
When man makes his unity with Spirit, his mystic
at-one-ment with his Father-Source, he finds his
unity with all creation. His life, seen correctly, becomes one unified, harmonious whole; for to see a
thing—whether animal, vegetable, mineral, or human—correctly is to be in league with it.

Disagreement with anything in the universal
Mind can only be the result of a false concept. All
things in themselves are divine ideas, and to be a part
of the one Mind is to be in harmony with its mani-

festations. In other words, it is to be in heaven,
which is the unity of all the units composing the
Universal.

When the race becomes thus unified it will grow
powerful beyond our present capacity to understand.
We are limited only by our present ability to comprehend and work with one another. We are shut
away from power because we do not think and act
in terms of wholeness. We fail in life because we
do not grasp life's racial unity, and, not seeing the
whole, we do not discern our individual position and
relationship, either to that whole or to the individuals that compose it. To perceive this plainly would
enable us to have clear purposeful motives. It rests
within the power of each of us to see life as it really
is, and to rejoice in its exquisite beauty.

Nature maintains no boundary lines, recognizes
no isolation or detachment; where one country ends
and another begins is a matter of indifference to her.
The earth, not just a bit of soil, supplies man with
sustenance; the sun, not just a few detached sun rays,
gives him vitality. But man has hedged his individuality about with all sorts of limitations. Family
ties, business methods, exaggerated patriotic sentiments, have become barriers to his complete freedom. In the egotism of self-conceit he has magni-
fied his intellect or his possessions until he has lost
sight of the universal Mind of which he is but a
part, and of the divine substance of which his portion
is but a single manifestation. His maps are not large
enough, his ideas are not comprehensive enough.

Fixing his attention on the whole, and on his relationship to it, will restore his sense of proportion and will set him free from the limitations of his little self by releasing his divine individuality and its vast possibilities.

Goethe says that on every height there lies repose. We know this to be true, whether it be in the contemplation of a mere physical range of vision, or in the peace of spirit accompanying freedom from the petty limitations of everyday living. Gazing at the magnificent panorama visible from a mountain-top, the eyes are freed from neighboring obstructions and focused to behold all, instead of various parts. Boundary lines disappear; objects merge into the landscape and are lost in the vast expanse of totality.

Just so, spiritual heights reveal beauties hitherto unseen, and erase the boundary lines that man has drawn around himself to separate and isolate his human individuality. For no man may live unto himself alone. Even before he is born he is dependent on another life for his physical sustenance, and this dependence increases and extends with his material growth.

Man's spiritual, or second, birth releases him from reliance on things material, by bringing him into a knowledge of his soul's unity with God, wherein he will find immortal freedom. Bringing men into this spiritual birth was Jesus' idea of glorifying His life and crowning it with success. It was the object of His last prayer for those whom He loved best—the prayer that they might understand that unity of spirit in which man realizes his oneness with his Creator, and with all creation. He saw, so very clearly, that in this way only the kingdom of heaven could be established among men!

Disagreement, disorganization, division, all indicate a sense of separation, and what are death and hell but a sense of separateness, of being cut off, detached, from the whole? The Nazarene saw disunion as the great destroyer that brought every kingdom to desolation, every city or house or person to certain failure. We know this to be as true today as it was two thousand years ago. More and more is the world accepting and seeking to apply the principle of unity, which strengthens every department of living.

Beginning with himself, man may respond to the urge of this principle that he is one with the Father. This response is his acceptance of his inheritance of "all things whatsoever the Father hath"—of the one mind, the one life, the one love, the one substance, common to all men alike. But it is not enough to respond to and accept the principle. The power of unity lies in its continuous practice.

Unity denotes agreement, harmony, oneness. How much of it do we practice in our lives? How strong is our unity of spirit to establish the bond of peace within heart and mind? Are we agreeing with good, co-operating with it, making it our own? Are we agreeing with our fellow men, working with them, claiming our friendly relationship with them? If so, we are fulfilling the two great command-

ments upon which the whole law hangs. For the
great and first commandment of the Teacher was to
love God with the entire being, and the second was
like unto the first in importance—to love mankind
as we love the individual self of man.

To be at variance with our fellow men is to deny
ourselves that bond of spirit which is the foundation
of all companionship, all friendship, all peace of
mind. To let any old, unhappy ghost of resentment
lurk in the depths of memory and push us away from
one or more of humankind is to raise a barrier between ourselves and our divine nature. "First be
reconciled to thy brother, and then come and offer
thy gift," to the Universal.

Every group of individuals, whether it be family,
school, business, church, or nation, seen in terms of
totality, becomes a thing of progress, because each
unit exists on account of its agreement with others.
The child who will not conform to family life is always in difficulty. At school, if he cares for ath-
letics, the first thing required of him is teamwork;
for no matter how brilliantly he may play the game,
if he does not do so impersonally and unselfishly, for
the welfare of the team, his contribution means little.

In the business world men are coming to realize
that co-operation is better than competition; that
mutuality should be the dominant principle; that injury to another is bound to react in injury to self,
because injury in either case is one and the same
thing. What is true of an injury is true also of a
benefit; therefore the psychology of success lies in

taking thought *for* others instead of in taking advantage *of* them. The old law of business transactions, the striving to get the better of the bargain, is becoming null and void as men are learning the benefits of a practical application of the Golden Rule.

More than ever before in the history of the world, men are crying for peace. The world's enlightened leaders are urging reciprocity, which is but another way of saying "unity." Our own country—these United States—seeks to pass on the ideal of its forefathers, that "union is strength," and that liberty and union are one and inseparable, now and forever, whether applied to a nation or to an entire universe.

The cardinal doctrine of the Christian church certainly should be spiritual unity, yet we know that such unity is not practiced. Many religious leaders continue to lay more stress on the virgin birth than on the rebirth of spirit. Inclosing their little maps in the creed and dogma of denominational baptism and ritualistic communion service, they fail to realize that the spiritual baptism and communion for which the church forms stand are often wholly lacking in the minds of those who conscientiously observe their teaching.

That the normal condition of the church is unity, most of its members agree. That the establishment of unity is a necessary issue is obvious. All denominations are demanding it, yet none of them seems willing to change those human opinions which obscure reality and which split the real issue on the

rock of ritualistic creed. Truth is a unifier, yet it is
no secret that denominational discord has driven
thousands of people away from church affiliation.
Discord based on dogma is the great enemy standing
in the way of the foreign missionary. I was told recently of one such leader who, because he understood
and practiced Christian unity in his work in an Afri-
can mission, was called home to face a church tribunal. His trial resulted in his being reproved and
asked to retire from active service!

Is Christ divided? We deplore the fact that sec-
tarianism and antagonism have developed in the
camp of His disciples. There is but one church—
the Universal Triumphant Church, founded on the
consciousness of Peter, which is faith. We are ini-
tiated into this church through our sense of unity
with that faith-consciousness. No other requirement
is necessary for membership.

I am often asked if the Unity movement is a sect
or an organized denomination. It is not. A sect
implies a part of something, a faction, whereas unity
is a union of parts a oneness so complete that separateness is impossible.

The great educational and healing movement
that we designate by the name of Unity is based on
revelation or perception, of Truth. It rests on the
Christian foundation of the fatherhood of God and
the brotherhood of man. It recognizes all members of the human family as brothers, because they
are all children of the one Father. It seeks to incor-
porate in its teaching the Truth-germ of every de-

nomination. It includes every such revelation of every age. Its maps are not inclosed in the boundary lines of limited human beliefs. Theologians would have us believe that only in the Scriptures is divine Truth set forth; that all other sources of knowledge are profane in comparison, and lack the quality of sacredness. Is not *all* Truth sacred, and *all* revelation divine?

Unity's maps are vistas of Truth, in which divine intelligence, incarnated as Buddha, merges with the mystic Tao of Confucius; in which a stern Jehovah of the ancient Hebrew prophets blends with the tender Fatherhood that Jesus taught. Included in these vistas, these highroads of revelation, are all expressions of eternal verity, whether of art or of science, of philosophy or of religion; whether ancient or modern, from Greece or Rome, from India or China; whether of Paul or Apollos or Jesus. All great minds of all civilizations and of all times have contributed their gifts to Truth; these gifts are but their perceptions of the one unchangeable, universal Truth, of which each individual expression is a part. For Truth is one, just as Mind is one, and all its revelations are grounded in the Spirit of truth, which shall lead man into *all* Truth.

Unity is more than a movement—it is a universal principle, the perception and self-application of which change man's consciousness and revolutionize his living. Unity is man's opportunity to co-operate with God.

"That they may all be one." How far men have

wandered from this ideal! And how they have
suffered in their wanderings! How hideous have
been the results of their disagreements and dissen-
sions! How their little boundary lines of prejudice
and greed and hatred have cramped and embittered
their lives!

Friends, "we must study larger maps." Maps
with extended boundaries, wherein tolerance over-
laps prejudice, unselfishness blots out greed, and love
overshadows hate. Maps whose regions are an inheritance common to all mankind, and whose inher-
itors are all of one family—the royal family of God.
The law of this larger land is order and harmony,
and its ruler is our loving Father, always inviting the
co-operation of His children. The royal temple in
which He dwells is not in some far-off province, but
close at hand—in the very heart of each of His subjects. He lives, loves, thinks, and speaks through
them, and manifests Himself in their lives as they
agree with, and release in themselves, His beneficent
power.

Somewhere, in each individual, there is a free
avenue for the universal Soul. To find that way of
the universal Soul through ourselves is to find the
essential idea that is our particular expression of
the whole. Universal unity is the direct outreaching
of each human unity to enter into right relationship
with the source of its own being, and with the other
units of which the race is composed.

There is but one life, of which yours and mine
are but parts—life unlimited and everlasting, which

the Christ consciousness in each man may lay down and take up, as it wills. There is but one love, which is ours to express—an all-encompassing love, excluding none. There is but one intelligence, for which each human mind is a broadcasting station. There is but one substance, which we may bring into manifestation through the Christ-recognition that named it according to the needs of those He served.

The Unity principle is not new. It is the same today as when Jesus taught it to an unheeding world. He did not originate it; He discovered it for Himself, just as you and I must each find and appropriate it. "Greater *works* than these shall he do," was His prophecy of him who should find it, and His prayer for racial unity has resounded throughout the ages:

"That they may all be one; even as thou, Father, art in me, and I in thee, that they also may be in us . . . And the glory which thou hast given me I have given unto them; that they may be one, even as we are one; I in them, and thou in me, that they may be perfected into one."

John 17

The Beginning and the Ending

THE GOSPEL STORY begins and ends with a Saviour whose saving or healing power is the fulfillment of Christianity. His existence upon the earthly plane was of such importance that it divided world history into two sections and marked the beginning of a new era of time. He brought not only a revelation but a revolution of thought into expression. Although He lived in a world governed by soldiers, He taught peace. The great Roman Empire was proud and haughty, but He urged humility. Men were cruel, false, and deceitful, but by His every word and act He proclaimed, "Be true!"

It seemed an impossible undertaking, this cleansing and healing of humanity, this establishing of a kingdom in the souls of men by a revelation of the nature of God as love. Very early in His ministry He began teaching and demonstrating an unheard-of principle, the law of love. To love God was the first of those commandments so jealously guarded by the theologians of the day. It was also first in the doctrine of Jesus, but to love mankind, although second in position, was to Him just as important, and these two commandments constituted His simple creed and comprised the entire law.

We cannot study the 5th chapter of Matthew without realizing that love practiced as the Master practiced it renders all other law unnecessary because it fulfills all law. It is no wonder that the

disciples caught the idea and made it the prime
factor in their work, or that Paul wrote around
it the most sublime love letter that has ever been
composed. To the Corinthian Church he tried to
recommend a panacea for every trouble that can
come to humanity. He concluded that only three
qualities "abide," faith, hope, love, but the greatest
of these is love.

Above all else, Jesus used His power to heal and
elevate human life. He knew that when a person is
weak and sick, when his body is racked with pain, he
has little joy in life, even though he may possess
every other means of material comfort. Today, even
though men still kill each other for greed and gain,
I am convinced that the law of love is advancing in
human relations. There are many who have sensed
the true meaning of the essential principle of the
Master's teaching and who have touched its infinitely constructive possibilities; who have found
that their experience of real happiness has come
through their radiation of the divine love to those
around them, through their unselfish service in alle-
viating the distress of the world.

To many it will seem strange and unusual to
classify love as spiritual health, closely connected
with physical wholeness. Few regard such an "intangible" thing as love as an attribute of bodily
healing. But the metaphysician sees it as a divine
radiation, whose release quickens the spirit, lifts the
life forces, and promotes physical soundness. This
idea should be easy to understand in this scientific

age, when the universe is rapidly being reduced to a system of vibratory force.

Love is good will in action. It holds the universe together by its constructive, dynamic, unifying power. It is the great solvent of every limitation and every problem; the one power transfusing itself through infinite channels. Modern man has learned a great deal about power, its application and control, but he is just beginning to realize that it begins and ends within himself, in his own mind. As dissipated energy is wasted energy, it should be his object to control and apply his power to the business of living.

Nothing gives one a greater realization of the power of thought than the knowledge that power constantly responds to man's will and that man has the ability to draw upon an inexhaustible reservoir of active energy at any time and in any place. Every day science is making discoveries proving that infinite forces of vitality do exist that have just begun to be utilized. Waves and radiations are no longer confined to the laboratory; they are fast becoming factors in our daily living. Eminent physicians are recognizing them in connection with the body, agreeing that the symphonic harmony of health depends on certain mental and bodily rhythms to which man may adjust himself individually.

The modern metaphysician prescribes thought vibration much as the physician treats disease by applying various heat and light and other rays. But there is this difference. The metaphysician substi-

tutes the primary elements of the "love spectrum,"
the various capacities of soul that must be used to
work with God to allow His fullness of power to be
manifested as a radiant expression of spiritual
healthfulness. He well knows that when these inherent capacities are used the body must respond
with a manifestation of the health that eternally
exists.

Healing is a natural result of energy liberated by
means of definite ideas. Health is, just as God is; it
needs only the opportunity to reveal itself freely and
fully as the boundless, changeless, irrepressible everlasting life of God, through His channel of expression: mankind. God's infinite life is love—life and
love are inseparable; for God is love. To be conscious of Him is to be conscious of love, and healing is the result of this consciousness of God. To
live consciously with Him and share His life one
must necessarily be a partaker of the divine nature,
where all life begins and in which it should ever
remain existent.

Healing is making whole, and wholeness suggests
restoration to an original, pre-existent completeness.
When we speak of being restored to health, we are
acknowledging it as an original, natural state of
being. According to Plato, "God holds the soul at-
tached to Himself by its root." To be rooted in divine love implies nourishment, growth, life. Paul
emphasizes this in his letter to the Ephesians: "He
would grant you according to the riches of his
glory, to be strengthened with might by his Spirit

in the inner man; that Christ may dwell in your hearts by faith; that ye, being rooted and grounded in love, may be able to comprehend . . . what *is* the breadth, and length, and depth, and height; and to know the love of Christ . . . that ye might be filled with all the fulness of God."

Paul is convinced that nothing, either "tribulation, or distress, or persecution, or . . . peril, or sword," can separate us from the love of Christ. He is "persuaded that neither death, nor life, nor . . . things present, nor things to come, nor height, nor depth, nor any other creature, shall be able to separate us from the love of God." We may use it as the key that opens the door to peace and happiness here and to perfect understanding hereafter. Love will solve every problem, and nothing in this world or any other can cut it off from us; for love is the master key that unlocks every door. It frees the imprisoned self and releases the individual powers. It is the key to every situation, banishing limitation and opening wide the door of spiritual healing.

Every person believes in love, but many understand it only on the material or physical plane. I am aware that it is one of the most baffling, elusive words in our language, used to indicate affection, passion, philanthropy, friendship, good will, and all manner of likes. It is decidedly not the erotic passion so many poets and novelists make of it—supremely selfish in motive and conduct—but a quality of Spirit. Although so difficult to define, although it has been misnamed, misunderstood, and misapplied, it remains the greatest power in the world, the very essence of well-being. Its power is inexhaustible, its possibilities unlimited.

The love I am speaking of is not dependent on anything in the outer; no person or condition need influence it. It is in itself a state of blessedness, because it is the essence of God and intimately connected with our life. Thought is the connecting link between it and the material world. Inspired by love, thought establishes higher radiations in the body, radiations productive of greater energy and more truly rhythmic.

The spirit of love crowds out of men's minds all sense of bitterness because of fancied wrongs; it sets aside all differences and opens wide the windows of the soul, letting the God within shine forth. If God is love, then love is all that God is. No person can love God without this love's outflowing toward all of God's children; therefore love is the constructive, unifying power that holds the universe together.

"A new commandment I give unto you, that ye love one another; even as I have loved you." This was almost the last injunction given by the Master to His disciples, and practicing it was to be a mark of identification. "By this shall all men know that ye are my disciples." Thus His teaching and His work met in one brilliant focus: the love that is the only panacea for the strife and inharmony of life.

Christianity fails to measure up to its mission if it cannot keep this supreme commandment. The principle of principles, the principle above every other, is love, which expresses itself in unselfish good will. If all Christians wore as a badge this principle of their Master, there would be no clash of creed and dogma, no greed of conquest, no bitterness of resentment. The meaning of Christianity lies not just in joining a church or subscribing to a creed. It is not in simply tolerating your fellow creatures. It is in being so filled with the love of all life as to feel responsible for it.

I realize the difficulty of loving those who lie and cheat, the stupid and the ignorant, the cruel and the unkind. But if we can, as Jesus did, look beyond ignorance and vice, back of lack and ugliness, past all erroneous thinking to the Christ Spirit inherent in every human being, we shall discover, as He did, the true reality that is each person's birthright. Jesus not only talked of this, He lived it. Recognizing the divinity of humanity, He loved and healed it.

There is no use in preaching love if we cannot practice it. Like a productive garden, man must yield his love for the benefit of others. He must give it out and relieve the lack that has fixed itself in the race consciousness and is expressing itself as evil conditions. For evil is a sense of lack. What is sickness but a lack of health, sorrow but a lack of joy, poverty but a lack of supply? Evil, then, is associated with lack, and lack is something that *is not.* Its opposite is goodness, wholeness, completeness, that which lacks nothing because it is all. If you would receive goodness, you must give it out as the loving service that desires to help others by making their burdens lighter.

The world, humanity, needs your services, and as you give them cheerfully and lovingly power gravitates to you. Loving service, this revelation of spiritual law that all can comprehend and apply, arouses new interest in the divine love that is God. To recognize this divine love is to make it a practical power in your life, for it is a constructive force, the secret of growth. It makes spiritual healing the most normal thing in life, the natural answer to the greatest and most importunate demand of the world, freedom from bodily suffering.

It is a mistaken idea that God ever "allows" sickness or suffering or that His will stands between it and its healing. "Thy will be done" is the prayer that Jesus taught His disciples, but this does not mean that God wills sickness, sorrow, or suffering for anyone. God's will is eternally good will. We repeat that God is love. Even imperfect human love does not will misery or pain. How much greater is the desire of divine love to bless and heal! It is not God's will that man should break the law of life and bring suffering upon himself by branding his body with the race consciousness of disease and death. We must know God as the principle of eternal love, in which there is no recognition of evil or error. God is love and love is God, and our "dis-ease," both mental and physical, arises from our act of rebellion in seceding from that universal love which includes all knowledge, all truth, all blessedness, all life, the greatest of the things that "abide," the healing power that never fails—love.

In his "Symposium" Plato gives a comprehensive idea of the love that "fills men with affection, and takes away their disaffection, making them meet together [in brotherly comradeship] . . . supplying kindness and banishing unkindness, giving friendship and forgiving enmity, the joy of the good, the wonder of the wise, the amazement of the gods; desired by those who have no part in him, and precious to those who have the better part in him . . . regardful of the good, regardless of the evil. In every word, work, wish, fear [it becomes] pilot, comrade, helper, savior. [It is the] glory of gods and men, leader best and brightest: in whose footsteps let every man follow."

In the words of the Master, who knew well the healing power of the love that is the fulfilling of the law, I end this work: "A new commandment I give unto you, that ye love one another; even as I have loved you, that ye also love one another."

PRINTED U.S.A.

4-D-10M-6-67